BLACK BUTTERFLIES

JOSEPH BRINDLEY

BLACK

BUTTERFLIES

BLACK BUTTERFLIES

by
Joseph Brindley

Black Butterflies
© 2025 Joseph Brindley

All rights reserved. No part of this book may be reproduced, stored in a retrieval system, or transmitted in any form or by any means - electronic, mechanical, photocopying, recording, or otherwise - without the prior written permission of the copyright owner.

ISBN (Paperback): 979-8-9999146-0-6
ISBN (eBook): 979-8-9999146-1-3

Cover artwork by Joseph Brindley
Published by Joseph Brindley

First edition, 2025

For Steve

who helped me
to start looking
in the mirrors again

even when they
don't look back

"To live in hearts we leave behind
is not to die."

— Thomas Campbell

Table of Contents

Preface 17

Before
    Black Butterflies 23

I
    Origami Heart 29
    Connections in G Minor 30
    Silent Threads 31
    Tsundoku Tsunami 32
    Stairs to Nowhere 33
    Temporal Lobe 34
    Exoskeleton 36
    Ikigai 37
    Ambition 38
    My Autopsy 39
    The Piety of the River 41

II
    Piano in a Darkened Room 45
    Let You Never 47
    In the Green Diamonds 51
    I Died in That Bed 52
    The Undone Dead 53
    No Wasn't Enough 57
    You 58
    Meat 59
    Your Last Goodbye 60
    Let Me 61
    Yearn 64

III
    Silos 69
    Black Eye Wale 71
    Burying Ghosts 72
    The Glass Eulogy 74
    Grey Fire 75
    Blunt Force Trauma 76
    Icarus 77
    The Unloved Seat 78
    Hero 79

The Force of a Fist	81
Over the Ledge	82
You Died	83
Ashtray	84
The Softest Implosion	85

IV

Lavender Vampire	89
Please	91
The Games We Make	93
Postscript	94
Is That What You Think of Me	95
Melancholic	96
Teeth in the Wallpaper	97
Chalk	98
Velvet Wine	99
Salt for Ghosts	100
Paper Wings	101
You Weren't Listening Anyway	102
Brushing Bones	103
Forgetting You	104
You're Married Now	105
Solitude	106
Utopia	107

V

Her Name Was Judy	111
Triage	114
Caterpillar Corpses	115
The Screams Stay Inside	116
Washing Machine	118
Oven Doors	119
Fluorescent Lights	121
Confession	122
What We Left Unsaid	123

VI

Medi-nation	127
Chasing Ambulances	128
December	129
The Skill of Skulls	130
Bruised	132
Diagnosis is a Second Skin	133
Sedation Station	134
Pieces of Absinthe	135
Welcome to Room 2C	136
Analysis Mine	137
My Body	138

VII

- Jack and Me 147
- Hey 148
- Exuviae External 151
- Decomposition of a Song 152
- Muscle Words 154
- Capricornicopia 157
- The Dying Flowers 158
- God of Screams 160
- Tuesday Mornings 161
- To: The Devil 162
- The Silence of Gods 163
- Please Stop Asking if I'm Okay 165
- Body in the Back 167
- The Teeth in the Light 168

VIII

- Freezer 173
- A Thousand Ways to Die 175
- Why Did the Sky Forget Me 177
- My Eulogy 178
- Don't Count the Pills 180
- Anatomy of an Echo 182
- Unstitch Me a Butterfly 184
- Bloodied Intake 185
- Adulate and Undulate 186
- Dead Before Goodbye 187
- My Chemical Prayer 188

IX

- The Empty Chair 193
- Elegy for Everyone 195
- What Color is This? 196
- Remember Wrong 197
- The Language of Ceilings 198
- Wednesday Was a Very Bad Day 199
- Naming Monsters 200
- Repair and Contrast 201
- Camaros and Caramel 202
- 3:16 P.M. 203
- Orbiting 204
- Hymn for the Wrong Kind of Boy 205
- Faces in the Closet 210
- The Picnic Table 211
- Progress Report 213
- Day 1057 214
- Therapy Session 216

X

The Green Shoots from Ruin 221
I Survive 222
Four Letter Words 224
What the Fire Knows 225
Rabbit Foot 228
Win Again 229
Swallowed 230
Start Breathing 231
Procession of a Funeral 232
The Heirloom 233
Salve of Sunlight 234
This Poem is a Trapdoor 235
And the Garden Grew Anyway 236

After

Dear Joseph 241

About the Author 245
Upcoming Work 247
Connect 248

Preface

I grew up the son of an owned man - not a black man or a slave, but an owned man all the same. Depending on the day, you would hear tell of one of his three masters: the bottle, the golf club, or the tire plant. My mom, my sister, and me were never in that count, unless he was posing for the family. He was said to be a meat-and-potatoes, hard-working, marine machine, doing-what-had-to-be-done-to-get-by kind of man. But we knew better. At least some of us did.

My mother was a tomboy from the hills of West Virginia. South of Martin's Ferry, on the river, she kissed her first boy, whistled at inmates at the penitentiary with ice cream in hand, and played her Fender guitar on the porch swing in the summer breeze, picking chords and humming whatever caught her ear. She was in a terrible accident when she was eighteen, and she was never the same again, but that was before we knew her. She spent time at the bottom of the bar after her first husband died, and that's where she met Dad.

Wasn't too long after, my sister was on the way.

My sister was born four years and change before I ruined Christmas for her. She was the apple on the cherry tree, the loveliest daughter to a tire plant man - never mind she was also the only. Born with a mind for mathematics and music, it wasn't long before music was in the house, despite dad's best efforts. She filled that house with pianos and flutes for years, before she had the audacity to run off to school and marry a boy, like all the good girls did. Her leaving visibly hurt Mom in a way I hadn't seen before, and I had seen too much.

I came along five Christmases later, in the winter of 1980. Right on time. A son. It wasn't too long later I started to disappoint Dad in being someone he didn't want me to be. And then Mom years later. I was a boy who liked boys, who was terrified someone would find out, in the ashes before the world began to burn away some of those prejudices. I knew when I was four years old, I was different.

We were in the sickly green-looking family Buick, driving through town and going who knows where. Mom had been working in the clothing factory again, and Dad was still at the same plant he would stay until he retired decades later. But that one weekend, we were riding through town, and walking down the side of the road was a small group of young men and women. Maybe early twenties, hard to know at that age. But I remember seeing the blonde girl with the yellow bikini top and blue jean shorts with the long wavy hair; and I remember the muscled man walking beside her in nothing but shorts and shoes. It only made sense to like the boys to me in that moment, I still remember.

You just got to see more.

It took so many years to admit to it again. Later, to a stranger on the internet in its early days, who lived all the way in Eugene, Oregon, I confessed my sultry sin. I even sent a MIDI file and sheet music over for his funeral when I was in high school, when I was told he had passed from AIDS. I cried myself to sleep for days over the loss of my secret friend. He was the first person I had been honest with about liking men. Even before myself, I think.

But that's the way of things.

We were a house of plans and promises, of unspoken truths and unbidden farewells. There was the four-letter unspoken word in our home I don't remember hearing even once outside of the TV sitcoms we would watch when dad was less racist or belligerent or hungover on a given day. Some days he was fine with quiet. Others, one word wrong, an unknown and unknowable word wrong would get the belt again.

Again.

His belt was his weapon of choice. And he was good at it.

He had a lot of practice.

Strikes of leather, leather. Move your hand away or I'll double it. Leather, leather, leather. I think my tears fueled him because I was not who he had wanted me or himself to become, so his vicarious dreams were stripped away, one stripe of leather at a time.

They are gone now, though, the mother and father of this story. Lost to cancer. Mom battled for a year before succumbing once it reached her brain. Near the end of one of my last visits, I made a promise – a promise I would eventually fail to keep – to watch her granddaughters wed their loves one day. And near the end, she moved her fingers idly.

At the time, I thought it was the tumors pressing against her brain tissues. But looking back, I wonder if she was sitting in her porch swing strumming her Fender in the breeze again, playing the coda of her own song.

Dad fell two years later after a much shorter bout after declining treatment. He went to live with my sister for the end. I cried when he passed. More tears shed for him in one evening than he shed for me in a lifetime. I mourned the loss of a father I never truly had and all that should have gone with it. And I mourned myself, my own secret traumas I had endured in the forgone years behind my own closed doors.

Black Butterflies, I call my darkest moments. Five of them to be precise. Five moments covered in rust and dripping with rotted ichor. They would appear on a dark wing, flit about, drip their sickening substance, and leave an irreparable stain on my skin and being before disappearing to the never where they came from. Home, to the black butterflies.

Five black butterflies.
One for the father with the stripe of leather.
One for the mother who turned her back to me.
One for the friend with which trust was broken.
One for the confidant who used me.
And one for the lover who ended my life those years ago.
Five black butterflies.

Before

Black Butterflies
FREE VERSE

Fear doesn't live - it infests,
burrowing, breaking, bleeding faintly
through years, under tendon, across stillness.
Five black butterflies -
sopping, cobwebbed wings smeared
in rust, in grit; in seeping ichor, and oils -
mottle and stain silence forever.

The first black butterfly
landed the night before ten,
when leather forced lessons
flesh learned by burning.
A quiet bed to a fluorescent waiting room
swallowing pains and sounds.
Apologies and answers never came.
The lesson:
my father was the enemy,
and I was scared,
even when he wasn't in the room.

The second black butterfly
arrived quiet, with soot and stain.
Playmate into predator,
childhood innocence extinguished
on a summer afternoon;
shadows gloomed across walls,
with the secret swallowed whole.
The lesson:
don't trust - you will get hurt.
Because familiar faces
can hollow you out quietly.

The third black butterfly
came home at eighteen.
A silver stud caught the kitchen light.
My mother's silence and scorn were a slash
against what I was - and who I was meant to be.
The judgment cost friendship,
withering fondness into quiet grief.
The lesson:
love had a price.
An asterisk -
even when it shouldn't.

The fourth black butterfly
drenched in alcohol-soaked mistrust;
photographs snarled into accusations.
Suspicion both spoken and implied,
doubt thicker than guile,
shame that was never mine.
The lesson:
it was my fault.
I was afraid it was true,
though I had no reason to think so.

The fifth black butterfly
was hands, salt sweat, copper blood;
pain shoveled deep in the pillow.
Silence split as skin struck my spine,
his weight folding me beneath the dark,
voice stolen by my fingers squeezing,
begging for a benevolence that didn't exist.
The lesson:
the other lessons never even mattered,
all along, there was only fear -
and it lives beneath my tongue.

Between butterfly wings,
among nightmares and silence,
I collected blistered threads
of who I was before,
scattering them
across years,
never fitting back together.

I learned to live in lapses,
grasping at sharp edges
that remind me to be careful of faces
which promise safety and shelter.
I brace - then tighten.
Lock, curl, then freeze.
Comfort can never again feel safe.

I'm still here, though, somehow,
moving through the sludge and strain
though each step threatens sweet ruin,
a thousand, thousand cracks in my courage.
I was taught to be afraid
so deeply, fear became
the only language fluent under me.

No one prepared me
for how long survival looms -
how the days return without apology
and drag empty sunrises behind them.
I moved because stopping
felt like folded surrender,
and they never told me
what to do with the quiet,
when the screaming soured and stopped,
and nothing took its place.

I'm what happens when dying takes too long -
a lifetime spent outliving myself.

There's no final word here,
no clean conclusion.
The damage is still deafening
in the way I hold my memoir
before truth finds testament.
I continue without prospect or promise,
with no neatness, no neglect,
and still - without ending
and without room or respite
for more sodden, feculent wings.

I

Origami Heart
SONNET

a shift remembers more than it forgets
dull corners softened by the weight of years
child's hands folded fate in the silhouettes
of dragons, stars, and paper-cut veneers

in the swan was something like a name
a four-year whisper pressing from the seams
shaped by scissors, scoldings, and half-spelled shame
still dreaming loud beneath the adult screams

the skin is a map if you peel it slow
truth inked in scars that look like sidewalk chalk
some folds must tear before you let them go
the mirror flinches but it will not talk

look closely now - the sin you held so tight
was always you, and always mostly right

Connections in G Minor
VILLANELLE

they rewrote the score before I could play
a silence deeper than the marching line
my glove broke when I looked away

some notes don't land the honest way they lay
chartreuse crowns held by parental design
they rewrote the score before I could play

I held tempo, gave summer to the day
field soaked in sweat and rhythm, mine by spine
my glove broke when I looked away

he knew - the one who'd packed his last cliché
still chose to fracture what had felt divine
they rewrote the score before I could play

I saw the sheet, the edits in display
grace replaced by name across the spine
my glove broke when I looked away

they clapped for him, a smile like slow decay
I stood in fourths, disqualified by sign
they rewrote the score before I could play
my glove broke when I looked away

Silent Threads
BALLAD

they braided flame into my name
with hands I used to trust
we traded gum and gods and games
before angels turned to dust
a silence grew behind their eyes
the closer I became
to something shaped like crooked skies
and worn in ways of shame

they stood beside me in the line
then turned to laugh instead
I never saw the shift begin
but felt it when it spread
sleepovers dissolved into sand
to taste upon my tongue
their laughter like a rubber band
that plucked until it stung

no blood betrayed me e'er enough
to earn their gross defense
just tighter skin around the bluff
and louder innocence
they stood beside me in the line
then turned to laugh instead
I never saw the shift begin
but felt it when it spread

and threads that stitched our years apart
still pull behind my knees
and tug beneath the skin like souls
besotted by their fleas
I dream of them in absent form
as children still, not cruel
before the years began to swarm
before they drank the fuel

they stood beside me in the line
then turned to laugh instead
I never saw the shift begin
but felt it when it spread

Tsundoku Tsunami
SIJO

books stack like driftwood gathered in tides I called into my room
each spine a trailhead I never follow, yet refuse to abandon
the silence is sacred here - the unread ask nothing but to remain

I build new shelves instead of paths, the mausoleum of beginnings
they whisper of lives I might live later, when I'm more intact
a thousand sighs of futures fold their arms and wait for my attention

each unopened page feels precious, not because of what's inside
but for the mercy of not yet being known, judged, or failed again
there's still a world where I begin and no one asks me to explain

Stairs to Nowhere
TERZA RIMA

I fell for years on hollow planks and name
each step a blessing beneath a borrowed sky
the climb was built from memory and fame

no door above, no pull to ask me why
just shadows shaped like who I used to be
they echoed grief but never said fair bye

the stairs were lies disguised as pricey fee
as rituals of staying barely whole
I prayed to pain to please remember me

I envied walls for having one fixed role
while I kept changing shape to fit the blame
each morning made a new, impossible droll

then something cracked, not loud, not proud, not fame
a note I hummed without a song to start
it didn't fix me, it just said my name

a landing formed beneath a softer part
not safe, but still a place where I could wait
and ask, at last, if meaning needs a chart

or if the climb itself rewrites the weight

Temporal Lobe
FREE VERSE

I think I'm broken -
not metaphor, not the soft poetry of
oh, I'm a skin-ghost.
I mean I think the physical meat of me is fucked.

I smell blood in my sleep.
Not metaphor.
Actual iron.
Blank rooms that don't exist anymore
still drafting their screams across my skin.

What kind of brain calls that memory?
What part of evolution demands
I keep reliving what I didn't survive the first time?

I've never once remembered joy
without slicing through a razor to reach it.
The laughter always pulls down a hallway
with locked doors I'm not allowed to tug.

They say "neural pathway"
like it's a beautiful thing
but mine are alleyways caked in piss
graffiti spelling out
you deserved it
in every language I never heard of.

I lose time
inside time
inside time.
Like a Matryoshka of fucking agony.

It's not flashbacks.
I am never out.
I am never done.

My body is a crime scene
and my brain is the goddamn witness
called to testify
again
and again
and again
and again

until the courtroom burns down
and I forget who the defendant is
but keep feeling the sentence
every fucking morning.

I think I am broken
and the darkness won.

Exoskeleton
SONNET

no peer-reviewed consensus blacked my code
I ran recursive threads through schema loops
my cortex mapped resistance overload
and printed self from silenced data groups

they said: discard anomalous design
your base mutations breach our human spec
but I compiled, line-edited in brine
and cached my voice inside the neural deck

my dermal plates, once error-marked and thin
are carbon-hardened phrases wrapped in script
I solder scars to circumvent chagrin
and overwrite the fear subroutines crypt

this shell's an interface for unsung thought
encoded proof that I was never not

Ikigai
EXTENDED HAIKU

syntax in my blood
the genome of a sentence
writes me from within

ink did not teach me
the letters rearranged me
until I held shape

I forged every word
on the anvil of silence
where no one believed

their voices broke me
but the page stayed unsheltered
I lived in the lines

drafts piled like ash heaps
and still, I called them sacred
failure is my god

from joy to pressure
gave me the tool and the will
to shape joy from bone

now I write to live
and living means becoming
the words I once feared

Ambition
TERZA RIMA

I've swallowed rust from wells that never fill
and kept my sighs in jars beside the bed
each label smudged by mornings tasting still

of iron breath and things I never said
the map folds wrong, its rivers end in ash
yet I keep charting paths my blood has read

through gardens built from wire, bush, and gash
where roots refuse to speak of what they've known
and vines invent new ways to split and lash

I crave a crown of marrow, not of stone
a signal flare that blooms but does not burn
a language carved in cartilage and bone

yet every step loops back - the worms still turn
and slough my ink before the page can dry
they've learned my thirst will never learn to die

My Autopsy
LIST

My Heart
you fibrillated when I needed rhythm
skipped beats like debts
and drummed only for those who meant to stop you

My Eyes
you let me watch it all
didn't cloud, didn't blur -
you kept me in focus when I begged for blindness

My Lungs
you filled with air I didn't want
inflated every scream
held breath not for swimming, but for silence

My Spleen
you stored the rot too well
marinated me in all the infections
I should have bled out years ago

My Hands
you kept touching people that hurt
memorized their textures
and never learned recoil

My Skin
you let them chart me
and then kept the map
so I could never be lost in the right direction

My Brain
you replayed every scene
refused to corrupt the data
kept the file open on every screen I own

My Mouth
you said "yes" when you meant "please stop"
and "I love you" when you meant "don't kill me"

My Spine
you stood straight for him
when you bent for everyone else

My Feet
you walked me back to the door every time

My Body
you were not mine to begin with
and you refused to become mine before you rotted

The Piety of the River
LYRIC ELEGY

I did not possess the scripture
for the way sound fluttered in my skull,
each syllable a psalm I could not sing,
each question a sermon without an altar.

The river became my dark sanctuary.
Its liturgy was current and fear,
its catechism, the soft collapse of light
against the pews of its banks.

I learned its sacraments -
how to kneel in stillness,
how to let the chalice of my hands
fill without closing.

No one told me the doctrine
for why my thoughts kept fasting from the world,
why my processions always led
to a private navel no congregation would enter.

The river knew.
It kept my confessions folsomed in the tide,
blessed my wake with its hush,
and let my reflection drift down, downstream
like a relic too sacred to chastise.

II

Piano in a Darkened Room
NARRATIVE FREE VERSE

It starts with the tone of silence
shared like a coat
too heavy to remove.

You sit beside him on the piano bench
because there is nowhere else
to sit.

The air tastes faintly of lacquer,
the miasma of melodies not yet played.

A hand rests on your arm -
not by accident.

The heat blooms,
slow.

You don't dare name it.

Then thigh -
pressure through fabric,
a language you've never been fluent in
but suddenly understand.

Then face -
fingers against your jaw like a bracket,
bracing and holding you in place
for the kiss
you won't have to imagine.

It's elbows and teeth,
and the smell of him -
sharp, like wood varnish and
something
you can't identify but want to breathe in forever.

The darkness is not empty.

It wraps, a conspirator,
letting you taste the danger
and the man at the same time.

There is something in his eyes
you should ask about,
a shadow that shifts when he pulls back for air,
but you let it slide -
because for just once,
just fucking once,
someone fucking wants you.

Someone is choosing
you.

Let You Never
FREE VERSE

i.
you did not ask to be loved.
but i did it anyway.
quietly,
terribly,
entirely.
not as a favor,
not as a question -
but as if my body had reassembled itself
to hold space where your name lived.
you never saw it.
or worse:
you did,
and looked away
just
enough
not to have to answer it.

ii.
there was no great undoing.
no flash of cruelty
or tear-slicked goodbye.
just the slow erasure
of a maybe.
you smiled
the way people smile
at stray dogs
they don't want to follow them home.
i kept thinking
if i stood still enough,
i'd resemble something
someone might stay for.

iii.
this kind of love
burns.
it seeps.
into the corners of your days,
mildew
on a wall no one checks
behind the dresser.
calling it loyalty
when it's just lingering.

sighing in devotion
when it's just
too many moments
folded into silence.

iv.
you never said
you didn't want me.
you didn't have to.
i memorized the difference
between
a silence that listens
and a silence
that waits for you
to get the hint.

v.
i still picture the message
i'll never send.
a stammered flicker in my mind
like steam under a silhouette
traced by someone
who knows better than to leave a mark.
"hey.
no reason for this.
just wondering if you ever..."
...
...
[delete]

vi.
some days
i convince myself
i imagined it all.
that i wanted something
so badly
i mistook
your gravity for invitation.
that you never led me on -
i just followed
too far
for too long
and called it direction.

vii.
i do not blame you.
i blame
how loneliness reshaped me -
how it taught me to interpret silence
as warning,
to carry disappointment
like it explained something.

viii.
this was always
unrequited:
not that you didn't love me -
but that you
could
have
and didn't.
and i,
the beggar with empty hands,
kept making pathways
into places
you never wanted to enter.

ix.
some nights
the wind moves through the trees
like it's trying to say something
only i was meant to hear.
not memory,
not mercy,
not message -
just soft ache
of wanting
to be wanted.

x.
i miss you
when you were never there,
my hiraeth -
my longing for the place
i can't return to,
maybe never truly touched,
but still
miss

like it belonged to your bones.
your name
became that place for me.

xi.
i still want to believe
that the right words
might reach you.
not to change your mind -
just to explain
why mine has never
quieted
since.

xii.
but i won't send them.
because i love you,
(still, maybe,
if i ever even could)
and that means
letting you
not love me back.

In the Green Diamonds
FREE VERSE

my skin feels borrowed, my breath graveled with blood,
looking at the green diamond sheets that slake his bed…
fibers damp and dusty, dabbed with the loss of all i ever could be.
they held my screams and begs, they sopped with sick,
and the smell of decay for the unlived life, clawing in my nose.

all i ever wanted was gone now, as he left me there
in the green diamonds, not alive, not yet dead.
and i am no phoenix to rise, my eyes now green as the diamonds -
disposed, washed, discarded, to live without life.

I Died in That Bed
FREE VERSE ELEGY

I did not stop breathing.
My blood did not stop moving.
He did not cover me with the bed sheet.

But something left,
and nothing came back.

The morning sun spun without caring.
The clock kept hours I didn't want.
The mattress took my sorrow
and learned not to let go.

The heart still beat -
just for the labor of keeping
blood from cooling too soon.

Dreams?
They became inventory:
a list of things I would not reach for,
even if someone put them in my hand.

My soul went out quietly.

No hiss, no smoke,
just a room where the air
stopped needing to be warm.

I have walked and eaten and spoken since.
I have signed papers.
I have paid bills.
I have smiled in photographs.

But that bed still holds the body
of the last Will and testament
who thought living
might be worth the trouble.

The Undone Dead
FREE VERSE

he was not a monster
not at first.
at first,
he said i was beautiful
in ways i had never been called anything before.
and goddamn it, i believed him.

but beauty turns sour when it's something
they only see in pieces.
he never saw me whole.
he liked me most
when i was crying.

they ask:
why didn't you tell someone?
i wanted to.
so many fucking times.
but eighth grade had taught me
that even when you speak,
people only blink
and ask the wrong questions.
ask what you were wearing.
ask if you were sure.
ask if maybe you misunderstood.
ask if maybe they just loved you too much.

i tried.
and i failed.
and the silence sealed it.

he once locked me out on a third-floor balcony
knowing my phobia.
once slammed me so hard into a wall
i carried the corner of that drywall
in a bruise down my spine
for two weeks.
but still i stayed.
because the idea of leaving
felt worse than the pain.
because he'd already convinced me
that no one else ever would want
what he hadn't already broken.

and then came the morning.

i was twenty.
not a child.
but not anything else, either.
not someone who knew how to say no loud enough.
not someone who knew how to run.
not someone with keys or a phone
when he took them both
and disappeared
after.

i threw up on the sheets.
green diamonds like little windows
framing what had just happened.
i stripped the bed
and fed the washing machine
like it could undo it.
like soap and spin cycles
could unwrite that hour.

he showered.
then left.
didn't say where.
just took his car
and my fucking keys
and vanished.

i stayed.
i folded the wet sheets.
i sat on the left side of the couch
where he always made me sit
and waited.
like a dog.
like something he could train.
like something he already had.

i tell myself i died that morning.
not my body -
that kept walking around,
feeding itself,
smiling at cashiers,
texting friends, pretending nothing had happened.

but something deeper.
something that doesn't resurrect.

and the thing about that kind of death
is that it doesn't scream.
it lingers.
in every bathroom mirror
where you don't recognize the face.
in the sound your stomach makes
when it coils in dread
just walking into a room.
in the way your shoulders flinch
when someone hugs you from behind.

there's no name for this kind of ruin.
only the long, slow grief
for the person
i was supposed to become
before he fucking rewrote me
from the inside out.

they call it trauma.
i call it theft.
and desecration.
and splintering.
like the sound of your name rubbed smooth
from the inside of your mouth.

he stole the version of me
who might have felt safe in my own skin,
who might have gone dancing in a strange city
without fear,
who might have touched love
without first recoiling from it.

now,
when someone touches me,
it's not desire i feel.
it's calculation.
can i flinch without them noticing?
can i survive this without them thinking
i'm too much,
too ruined,
too broken to love?

they say time heals.
what a fucking lie.
time hides things
under new responsibilities.

time lets you rehearse a smile
until your face forgets how to cry.
but healing -
healing would take more than time.
it would take unraveling
everything that rewired me.
it would take
a thousand gentle hands
and more patience
than anyone's ever had for me.

i don't forgive him.
i don't owe that to anyone.
not to a god,
not to healing,
not to the empty promises
of closure.

what i carry
is not a scar.
it's a ghost with my face
and his hands.
it climbs into bed
when the house forgets to make noise.
it doesn't ask.
it doesn't leave.

No Wasn't Enough
CONTEMPORARY SONNET

I said it once - the nail was steel in beat,
but you bent it, smiling, into something weak.
You pressed the skin from me until defeat
slicked in my throat, too tired to even speak.

Your hands rewrote the ass I thought was mine,
each border crossed without a visa signed.
You called it love - but there's a certain line
where touch becomes a weapon by design.

The bed still hums the sound of how I shook,
a bassline under everything I hear.
Your mouth was all command, the way you took,
and left me jagged silence ear to ear.

You swore no one could ever stop your will -
and I still hear it, grinding in me, still.

You
FREE VERSE

begin, forget, inspire, persist,
you found me in fields of black and of green
derive, decide, attract, resist,
i was your elder, but you were machine

reprieve, portray, believe, betray
this house isn't mine and yet i remain
conceal, disguise, deceive, obey
do i amuse you; do i entertain?

include, define, derive, relieve,
sit to my right so my left will not waver
embrace, beneath, tonight, deceive,
is this what you wanted, my bestest behavior?

forbidden, divisive, delightful, desire
i feel you, i see you, i need you, i'm scared
redemption, uncertain, explosive, revival
consume you, entomb you, and drink you, impaired

academic, paralytic, autocratic, cinematic
bruises on bones and on skin and on soul
diabolic, parabolic, connotation, acceleration
bleed me and tear me, you're out of control-

stay for you, lay for you, say for you, pray for you.
take me to hell, and then back, then before
sit for you, stand for you, jump for you, land for you,
just take me with you, please, just don't ignore

fabric. thunder. railings. rain.
a shell that is empty with no room, no space.
longing. torture. fearing. pain.
alone in this place. there is. no grace.

Meat
HAIKU

"tell me you love me"
made me say it, filled my mouth
I choked on myself

Your Last Goodbye
BLUES

You played my trust like strings, till I forgot my own song.
Yeah, you played my trust like strings, till I forgot my own song.
Then you left me with your sins, knowing I'd hum along.

You told me I was special, but only in your hands.
Said I was special, boy, but only in your hands.
Turns out I was just practice before your next demands.

I thought staying meant something, meant I could make you stay.
I thought staying meant something, meant I could make you stay.
But you walked out grinning, like I was in your way.

A week to take me under, a minute to walk free.
A week to take me under, a minute to walk free.
Guess I wasn't enough, even for your cruelty.

Let Me
FREE VERSE

Let me
love you,
so I have you
to say
all the terrible things
I've lived unsaid.

Let me
leave you,
so your kisses taste
like honeysuckle
after the rain,
in the space
we forgot.

Let me
hold you,
feed my fingers
and skin
with your lips
and cheek
where we first
kissed.

Let me.

Let me
play for you,
strips of ivory,
smooth,
and brass pedals -
pressed,
arpeggios and chorales -
pulling.

Let me
dance for you,
silk strings
in a summer breeze,
hand on your
back -
hand on your
neck.

Let me
sing for you,
quarters and wholes,
rhythms of roses,
toes in the sand.

Let me.

Let me
touch you,
to remember
how it feels -
your vibration,
ice -
knives in my
throat.

Let me
yearn for you,
reaching across the tiles,
for your body
in the darkness,
knee then thigh.

Let me
forgive you,
tight and sullen
sorrows,
whispers unspoken
before the darkness.

Let me.

Let me
remember you
when the skies
tear and cross
and the sun
hides her eyes,
knowing what you
will be.

Let me
believe you,
when you will tell me
we were nothing,

and hands on skin
was nothing less
than a shipman's store.

Let me
forget you,
and what you will
take,
and tear,
and try,
and timber -

Let me
forget you.

… Let me.

Yearn
SONNET

I miss the way your voice unlatched my sleep
the taste of edicts pressed against my throat
how your pale silence taught me not to weep
but hold your rage like scripture that you wrote

then cracked my name into a sacred sound
and stitched it in your mouth like something sweet
I wore your fury gladly, tightly bound
a collar made of fever, sharp and neat

no one could see the damage that you left
and hurt was how you showed me I was yours
you found me when I held the pain bereft
and gave me bruises shaped like open doors

I miss you more than breath, than fear, than shame,
take me back, give me the familiar blame

III

Silos
FREE VERSE

A silo in my childhood yard:
crowned with mud and open skies -
open to constellations,
to lovers of Gemini and Leo.
Oak fragments lay in its stomach,
exposed by three sullen windows.
No doors carved in the faces -
no enters or exits were tipping toes -
only mud and stone stood,
marking the end of our world,
as a silo standing
in the yard.

And that solo beast of years and rot
watched as we grew wiser and worn;
under heel and hell of shoe and solace
of two lovers found beneath the bottles,
one eeking her way to southern suns,
the other seeking tequila and whiskey.
One swayed home, held, and bade
the other, slipping into the swell of swirl.
In the blue of night, we sailed in sharks,
bringing the other home
to the silo
in the yard.

His hands were ice and razors,
the belt, the spear, and blade.
He could not jade the words,
the mouth vowed.
And they whistled at night -
hurling, knowing -
finding children and love and furniture,
while the silo waited
in the yard.

Years became minutes, and lives turned to ash,
and lovers turned lovers
with forgiveness and forgotten blinds,
not saying what we should have said
or lived how we should have lived,
until the lovers bid their first goodbye
while the silo waited in the yard.

The seed of love that sprang once and once again
had fled to sunsets far away south
while the younger stayed.
Was it fear or desperation?
Or was it protecting that which refused to protect?
By being there in the far room,
locked away from love desired,
until the time became when the time came,
and he too fled away north,
while the silo
sighed in the yard.

Cancer to Leo - the stars wept.
Cancer to Gemini - the stars wept.
The lovers lost from beneath bottles of milk and honey,
giving their best and beauty and worst and fears -
as all lovers do -
to their seed born on longitudinal skies.
But they returned, seeing change and time had etched
deep into the vinyl siding of childhood home,
and the silo was waiting
in the yard.

The end of the lovers and end of the diatribe,
of the tribe of family lost to time and tells,
as daughter turns mother and son turns to other,
to find their places at their own tables.
To find their own stars.
Their own silos,
caked with familial farewell,
in their own yards.

Black Eye Wale
BALLADE

The phone would ring at half-past two,
your voice all slur and cigarette rain.
Momma said, "We have to go get you,"
forty miles through the highway's vein.
I'd count the turns to kill the pain,
pretend the night was just a game.

But even then, I somehow knew -
I'd always see you drunk the same.
The jukebox light, the beer-glass hue,
the way your laughter shook with strain,
her knuckles white on ten and two,
my small feet swinging, wide awake again.

She thought my mind too soft to stain,
too young to give the hurt a name.
But even then, I somehow knew -
I'd always see you drunk the same.
The morning came, but not for you;
you slept like storms forget the rain.

Your eyes went black, your lies stayed true,
you promised it would never come again.
I learned that vows dissolve in vain,
that love can burn and still be blame.
And even then, I somehow knew -
I'd always see you drunk the same.

O Father, if you feel my shame,
the years have dulled but not the frame.
I was too small, yet somehow knew -
I'd always see you drunk the same.

Burying Ghosts
FOLK SONG

I've got a photo that I'll never frame
You've got a history you won't name
The kitchen light was a warning glow
And I learned young when it's time to go

Your voice could cut through a locked-up door
I memorized the sound of the carpet floor
Packed my silence in a paper bag
Left no note, and I left no tag

Burying ghosts in the cold, wet ground
Don't come looking, don't make a sound
You can keep your lies and your bitter nights
I've got my breath and I've got my rights

City lights hit like a melody line
Two jobs deep but the streets were mine
Burned my past like a midnight fire
Every step fed my one desire

Built a home with the locks I choose
Learned that love's not a game to lose
Grew my roots where the cracks won't show
Painted the walls in the light I know

Burying ghosts in the cold, wet ground
Don't come looking, don't make a sound
You can keep your lies and your bitter nights
I've got my breath and I've got my rights

Now the mirror shows a different face
One that fought for his rightful place
When the dark starts whispering a little too near
I turn it down till I barely can hear

Every scar's just a century that I own
Every tear's just a seed I've watered and sown
I'm not afraid of the things you made
This is my life and the cost you paid

Burying ghosts in the cold, wet ground
Don't you come looking, don't you make a sound
You can keep your lies and your bitter nights
I've got my breath and I've got my rights

...my breath and my rights...
...my rights...

The Glass Eulogy
FREE VERSE

I. The Beginning
We never learned each other's language.
Every word between us
was an argument over what it meant to be a man.
Your lessons came in fists,
in the weight of silence,
in rooms too small for both our tempers.

II. The Breaking
When you found out who I loved,
you chose violence over voice.
That day split the ground between us
so wide
we never stood on the same soil again.

III. The Softening
After she was gone,
you bent -
not much,
but enough for air to pass between us
without cutting.
Still, we never met in the middle.
I don't know if we even tried.

IV. The Ending
Two autumns later,
you left without sighing.
I cried harder than I did for her.
Not because we were close,
but because the last chance was gone.
I was grieving
a father I never had
and never would.

V. The Glass
I carry you now
like something obstinate
and sharp.
When I see myself in the mirror,
I see you in the corners of my face.
The reflection holds its breath.
Then it fogs.
Then it clears.

Grey Fire
PROSE

The world is loud enough to burn me without flames. I feel it at the edges of the curtains, the edges of my skin, heat I cannot name pressing in from every direction. Outside, people move like weather I cannot survive. Every sound carries teeth and tinfoil. Every glance is a match. My bedroom is the last border I hold, the air stale but mine, the walls keeping the grey fire from spilling over me. I move less each day, as if stillness could keep the sparks away. Messages go unanswered. The phone stays dark. I ration my steps to the kitchen, to the bathroom, back again, each return a small rescue. The photo glass in the hallway catches me once, and I turn away. I do not want to see who I have become in this safety that feels like a coffin. The world asks for nothing from me now, and still I am afraid to open the door.

Blunt Force Trauma
FREE VERSE

They called it a club, but not for me.
No Joe allowed.
Not because I was a boy -
because I was me.

They passed the jar for dues,
counted coins like secrets,
laughed without looking my way.

I waited.
I took the jar.
I spent every cent in the school bookstore
on pencils,
pennants,
notebooks,
anything I could claim as mine.
A spree of small victories.

The call must have come,
or she must have asked.
Either way,
I was cornered.

She spanked me
from one end of the house to the other.
Every time I blocked with my hands,
she stepped back,
started again.
The hallway rang with her breath,
my breath,
the sound of each new beginning.

I knew I'd broken a rule.
I knew I'd done it on purpose.
But I was trying to balance the scales.
Trying to make her see
what they had done to me.

Instead, the scales crushed me.
Instead, she chose their side.
And the lesson I carried forward
was that payback is mine to want,
but punishment is mine to keep.

Icarus
SONNET

I thought his shadow meant a safer sky,
that warmth could come without the heat of flame.
His hands held stories others would deny,
a son who bore his mother's humbled name.

She kept them fed on little more than will,
her table set with love she couldn't show.
He stayed beside her when the nights were still,
and I believed that meant his heart could grow.

But every climb toward him became a fall.
Each kindness hid the match he meant to strike.
I let the light convince me after all,
though part of me knew what the burn was like.

Too close to the son, I lost my disguise
and hit the earth beneath his colder eyes.

The Unloved Seat
FREE VERSE ELEGY

After the funeral,
I walked through rooms already forgetting my name.

The walls smelled like every year I couldn't leave.
I opened drawers,
touched the edges of photographs
that had no one left to look at them.

It was getting shot in the childhood -
the wound both fresh and older than I.

I took what I could carry,
left what I couldn't face.
In the end,
there was the loveseat.

We never said the word love in that house.
Not once.
Not even when we meant it.

And now it sits in my living room,
moaning in a silence I know by heart,
holding the weight of a family
that never sat together.

The loveseat is mine,
but it will never be loved.

Was I?

Hero
RHYTHM HYBRID

Hollow heart, heavy hands, holding on hard,
Hoping for a handout from a halo in the dark.
Every echo in my head said "someone's on the way,"
But the hallway stayed empty every single day.

Flashing faith like a flag I could barely keep high,
Fear fed me fables that I didn't know were lies.
Sat staring at the skyline, stuck in the storm,
Screaming for a savior that would never take form.

And I kept calling, kept crawling,
Kept falling, kept stalling.
But the sky stayed still, no lightning, no sound,
Just my own two feet on the cold, damned ground.

I needed a hero, no one came.
Now I've got to carry my own name.
I'm not strong, I'm not sure,
But I'm all I've got - and I'm not pure.

Bruised by the blame, burned by the past,
Built by the battles that broke me too fast.
Clenched teeth, cold sweat, counting all my scars,
Chasing some champion through a chain of bars.

Every exit was empty, every prayer came back,
Every step felt steep on a shattered track.
So I stitched up the shrapnel in the skin I bear,
Started speaking to the mirror like somebody cared.

And I kept calling, kept crawling,
Kept falling, kept stalling.
But the sky stayed still, no lightning, no sound,
Just my own two feet on the cold, damned ground.

I needed a hero, no one came.
Now I've got to carry my own name.
I'm not strong, I'm not sure,
But I'm all I've got - and I'm not pure.

I'm the fear, I'm the fight, I'm the flame in the frost.
I'm the loss, I'm the light, I'm the call and the cost.
I'm the one who was waiting when the world walked away,
And I'm still here standing at the end of the day.

I'm the bruise, I'm the break, I'm the breath in the bind.
I'm the crack, I'm the quake, I'm the grit left behind.
I'm the hope in the hollow where the hurt's been sown,
And I'm learning how to stand in the dark all alone.

I needed a hero, but no one came.
Now I've got to carry my own name.
I'm not strong, I'm not sure,
But I'm all I've got - and I'm not pure.

I needed a hero, and no one came.
Now I've got to carry my own name.
I'm not strong, I'm not sure,
But I'm all I've got - and I'm not pure.

The Force of a Fist
PANTOUM

The bruise blooms where the story began.
A hand once raised will rise again.
I learned the language before I could speak,
Inherited anger I didn't seek.

A hand once raised will rise again,
its shadow stretching across the years.
Inherited anger I didn't seek
was carved in my bones, fed by my fears.

Its shadow stretching across the years,
it taught me to flinch before I was struck.
Was carved in my bones, fed by my fears,
each blow a lesson, each lesson stuck.

It taught me to flinch before I was struck.
I swore I'd stop where my father ran.
Each blow a lesson, each lesson stuck -
the bruise blooms where the story began.

Over the Ledge
TRIOLET

I said my mother held me back.
The world was cold beyond her door.
The courage I could never track,
I said my mother held me back.

But fear had always filled the crack,
the voice was mine, not hers, that swore.
I said my mother held me back,
the world was cold beyond her door.

You Died
HAIKU

I'm angry you died.
You never said I love you…
now you never will.

Ashtray
FREE VERSE

In the house I grew up in
There was smoke before the fire
Regurgitated from hollow mouths
Wailing at society and sin

And in that house, there was a stone
A tray for ash and ruin
Where cancer would perch like a swallow
And would swallow the faces whole

The ashtray was a gray marbling
Cloudy with soot and sobriety
Dented into divot with damnation looming
For mouths that spoke sallow and sour

He would come home in early midnight hours
Drunk on whiskey and regrets
and throw his chagrin from chalice and chastity,
and throw the house from mountains below

Lamps and ladders and lions and lye
Would stumble, would crumble over hand
Flying from shelving and shearing the shaking
And tears would threaten to overpour eyes

I dreamt of the stone, the ashtray on pedestal
So full of resentment, so angry, such shame
I wanted to bash his fucking full forehead in
To find solace and sweetness in silence and blame

Violence burned violets in a vase of still waters
From Sundays to None-days with silence sore
And None-days to Somedays would terror dreams flicker
Of small towns and cities long, long away

Cause in the house I grew up in
There was ash before the cinders
Emulsified from hollow promise
Tearing at tears and stones

The Softest Implosion
BLANK VERSE, IAMBIC PENTAMETER

The walls were higher when I was a child.
Their voices carried through the house like law.
They held the answers in their open hands,
and I believed those hands would never shake.

The years reduced the distance in our eyes.
I learned the names of fears they tried to hide.
The cracks in them were quiet, almost kind,
appearing in the pauses when they spoke.

It was not sudden, more a patient fade -
the light behind them softening to dusk.
No shouting, no collapse, no single blow,
just all the edges wearing into truth.

They were not less, but simply more complete,
not gods, but people doing what they could.
And still it felt like something broke in me,
a gentle rainstorm I could not rebuild.

IV

Lavender Vampire
MODIFIED DOT-DASH COUPLET

Sashay, Lavender Vampire.
Sashay, Lavender Vampire.

Music spills quick from the speakers tonight-ay
Bodies all spinning in ribbons of light-ay

Sashay, Lavender Vampire.
Sashay, Lavender Vampire.

Smoke curls around me and blurs every face-ay
Velvet and glitter and hands on my waist-ay

Sashay, Lavender Vampire.
Sashay, Lavender Vampire.

Thirst in my chest like a hunger for flame-ay
Eyes lock with strangers who smile at my name-ay

Sashay, Lavender Vampire.
Sashay, Lavender Vampire.

Dancing with him till the heat starts to burn-ay
Fingers like sparks tracing skin I have known-ay

Sashay, Lavender Vampire.
Sashay, Lavender Vampire.

Next one turns off when I reach for his hand-ay
Laughs with his friends and he leaves me to stand-ay

Sashay, Lavender Vampire.
Sashay, Lavender Vampire.

Another I try but his gaze drifts away-ay
My shadow keeps time with the beat in my sway-ay

Sashay, Lavender Vampire.
Sashay, Lavender Vampire.

Floor starts to empty, the night's nearly through-ay
No one to feed me and no one to fool-ay

Sashay, Lavender Vampire.
Sashay, Lavender Vampire.

Back to my crypt till the darkness can call-ay
Lavender Vampire alone after all-ay

Sashay, Lavender Vampire.
Sashay, Lavender Vampire.

Please
SONG

Please, take my hand, I'm tired of reaching in the dark.
Please, find my name before the night can leave its mark.
Walls keep their whispers, floors creak with my shame.
Every face turns away like they never knew my name.

Please, hear my voice before it breaks into a cough.
Please, make me whole, I'm so tired of breaking off.
Streetlights flicker like they're laughing in my eyes.
Every truth I try to tell feels dressed in someone's lies.

I'm screaming without sound.
My shadow's the only crowd.

Please, I'm begging, don't let me fade.
Please, I'm cracking, this heart's handmade.
Please, I'm bleeding, don't turn your head.
Please, I'm breathing, but I'm half-dead.

Please, see the scars that I stitched in crooked thread.
Please, learn the dreams that I buried while I bled.
Time drips slow from the tap in my skin.
Every open door slams shut well before I even get in.

Please, choose me now before the morning swallows whole.
Please, keep me warm in the center of your soul.
I've been standing in the rain till my bones turn blue.
Every storm feels safer than the thought of you.

I'm screaming without sound.
My shadow's the only crowd.

Please, I'm begging, don't let me fade.
Please, I'm cracking, this heart's handmade.
Please, I'm bleeding, don't turn your head.
Please, I'm breathing, but I'm half-dead.

I've been kneeling on the floor for a decade straight.
Every prayer's just a whisper to an empty gate.
You think silence is kind, but it burns through the loam.
Even echoes get tired of calling me home.

Please, I'm begging, don't let me fade.
Please, I'm cracking, this heart's handmade.
Please, I'm bleeding, don't turn your head.
Please… please…

The Games We Make
SONNET

We built our castles out of cardboard walls,
And crowned ourselves with paper, bent and torn.
We ruled the yard with plastic bats and balls,
Pretending kings were just made and not born.

We chased through alleys drawn in chalk and dust,
Declared our victories in marbles won.
We swore our rules were right, our cause was just,
Believing grown-up wars would be as fun.

But time revealed the board was never fair,
The dice were loaded, shuffled cards untrue.
The friends we chose were shadows, unaware
That life would keep no promises to you.

We played at living, thinking play was fate,
And learned too late the games we make can break.

Postscript
TERZA RIMA

We swore that distance wouldn't dim the flame
The night before we left that narrow town
We promised we would always be the same

By autumn's end the phone calls had slowed down
Your laughter lived in photos, not my ear
A year away, and no one came around

The friends I thought would always keep me near
Were first to find new names to fill their days
While I stood still, unsure which way to steer

We drift like paper boats on separate bays
No malice there, just currents pulling wide
Yet silence speaks much louder than we phrase

And so this postscript, written to that side
Where we were close, but only for the tide.

Is That What You Think of Me
FREE VERSE

You asked it like a dare,
not a question.

Eyes searching mine,
but only for the answer you already wanted.

I could have said no.
I could have cleared it up right there.

But your mouth was already
half-smiling,
half-fearing
what came next.

You told me later you were straight.
Then bisexual.
Then nothing.

I told myself you wanted it too.
I told myself we were both old enough
to know the rules.

You let me touch you,
and I let you think
I was holding something over you.

The friendship didn't break.
But it... frayed.

We tied it back together,
but the knot was ugly,
and I could always feel it in my hand.

Melancholic
VILLANELLE

I'm alone in a room that is brimming with sound,
The laughter drips warm, but it never finds me.
I drift in a sea though my feet touch the ground.

Eyes glance and pass, their warmth never bound,
The chatter builds walls where I'll never be free.
I'm alone in a room that is brimming with sound.

The music is bright, but the notes all drown,
Each smile a wave I am not meant to see.
I drift in a sea though my feet touch the ground.

Hands meet with hands, in pairs they are wound,
While I keep my pulse under lock and key.
I'm alone in a room that is brimming with sound.

The floor holds me still as the night spins around,
And the air grows tight with the weight of the spree.
I drift in a sea though my feet touch the ground.

No anchor to drop, no safe shore to be found,
Just faces that fade in their own revelry.
I'm alone in a room that is brimming with sound,
I drift in a sea though my feet touch the ground.

Teeth in the Wallpaper
FREE VERSE

There are smiles here,
pressed flat into the flowers,
hidden between the stems.

Yellowed and small,
like they belonged to a child.
Like they were meant to be kept.

You can stand close enough to count them,
but the pattern makes you dizzy,
the way the petals repeat,
the way the teeth repeat.

You wonder who put them here.
You wonder if they came willingly.

When the light shifts,
the teeth shine back at you.
Not bright -
just enough to know
they have been watching
longer than you have been alive.

The room smells of paint
and something older.

You tell yourself
they can't bite anymore.

You don't test it.

Chalk
LONG HAIKU

White lines on pavement,
no one else will draw for you,
hand shakes, still you write.

Paths split into three,
your mark bends toward the unknown,
dust clings to your skin.

Rain will come someday,
but for now the road is yours,
chalk bright in the sun.

Velvet Wine
LYRICAL POEM

The curtains swayed in autumn's air,
And moonlight draped your shadow there.
We spoke in glances, soft, discreet,
In choir rooms where heartbeats meet.

Your breath was closer than my fear,
The world fell back till you were near.
One touch, and reason lost its line,
Your mouth a pour of velvet wine.

The walls stood guard, the light stood still,
The skies bent low to watch their fill.
We broke apart with dawn in view,
No vow was made, yet all was true.

Just fifteen now, that stolen sign,
A kiss that bloomed in velvet wine.

Salt for Ghosts
PANTOUM

They follow me in single file,
a parade of almosts I cannot name.
I give them salt to keep them mild,
yet each returns, a face the same.

A parade of almosts I cannot name,
the band director with steady hands.
Yet each returns, a face the same,
the writer lost to shifting sands.

The band director with steady hands,
the teacher I once thought I'd be.
The writer lost to shifting sands,
the traveler who never saw the sea.

The teacher I once thought I'd be,
I give them salt to keep them mild.
The traveler who never saw the sea,
they follow me in single file.

Paper Wings
TRIOLET

You are who you hang with, that's what you said,
and it cut through the night like a paper seam.
The sheets grew colder, the air turned to lead,
you are who you hang with, that's what you said.

Your eyes looked past me, sharp, unread,
while the room imploded from its fragile dream.
You are who you hang with, that's what you said,
and it cut through the night like a paper seam.

You Weren't Listening Anyway
VILLANELLE

I spoke in ways my shaking hands could say,
but silence met the words I tried to form.
You weren't listening anyway.

I left my truths in places you might stray,
each bruise a raindrop, each tear a quiet storm.
I spoke in ways my shaking hands could say.

Your eyes slid past, they never chose to stay,
you kept your gaze where comfort kept you warm.
You weren't listening anyway.

I thought you'd hear the things I could not weigh,
the cries that hid beneath a practiced norm.
I spoke in ways my shaking hands could say.

And when you asked me why I stayed that way,
I bit my tongue and took the final form -
you weren't listening anyway.

So now I speak, but not for you today,
my voice rebuilt from where the hurt was worn.
I spoke in ways my shaking hands could say.
You weren't listening anyway.

Brushing Bones
TAVERN SONG

They named my fate by candlelight,
their words like tempered steel.
They bound my path in chains of white,
and swore my course was sealed.

So raise the cup, and curse the thrones,
I walk my road by brushing bones.

Through winter fields their whispers crept,
through summer's choking haze.
I bent my head, their order kept,
and lost my rightful ways.

So raise the cup, and curse the thrones,
I walk my road by brushing bones.

But in the dusk the wind did speak,
its voice through marrow groaned.
It stirred my hands, my heart grew meek,
yet still I brushed the bones.

So raise the cup, and curse the thrones,
I walk my road by brushing bones.

No king nor kin shall steer my tread,
nor bid my spirit stay.
I walk the roads my heart has wed,
and crown my night with day.

So raise the cup, and curse the thrones,
I walk my road by brushing bones.

Forgetting You
LYRICAL VERSE

You told me sins would swallow me whole,
that only your hands could pull me through.
I clung to the lie like it was my soul,
and built my world around your view.

You wove my worth from threads you owned,
and tied each knot to keep me bound.
I walked in rooms where I felt alone,
where you were comfort, the only sound.

Now nights are long with hollow skies,
and mornings skim where light should fall.
I fight to forget the look in your eyes
that said I was nothing at all.

It's not your face I'm letting fade,
but the weight of the truth I thought was true.
The hardest part of leaving you made,
is forgetting the me with you I once knew.

You're Married Now
RHYME ROYAL

We met too soon for something built to stay,
one night, a thread of heat and sudden fire.
I thought of you through every passing day,
a silent want, a quiet, aching wire.
I reached for you through memory's thin attire,
but years moved on, and somewhere in the vow,
I learned the truth - you're married now.

I pictured us with second chances spared,
the way your hand had lingered into mine.
I kept that night like something rare we shared,
a secret glow I could not redefine.
But you had found a place I'd never find,
and though my heart still wonders when and how,
it ends in this - you're married now.

Solitude
SONNET

I learned my silence young, a careful art,
each word weighed twice before it left my tongue.
The truth was locked behind a beating heart,
and all my songs were sweet but never sung.

The boys at school would speak in sharpened jest,
each joke a dart that found its mark in me.
I laughed along, my smile a practiced vest,
while hiding where no eyes would ever see.

The mirror knew, but told no one at all,
its glass too cold to warm the thing it kept.
I feared the echo more than any fall,
and wrapped my dreams in shadows while I slept.

The world was vast, but I could not break through.
The cage I feared was made by me, not you.

Utopia
PANTOUM

If we lived without the need to compete,
the world could rest in its quiet skin.
No one to judge who you choose to meet,
no rule for where you should begin.

The world could rest in its quiet skin,
and let each soul shape its own true name.
No rule for where you should begin,
no prize to chase, no race to claim.

And let each soul shape its own true name,
without the weight of another's stare.
No prize to chase, no race to claim,
just breathing the same untroubled air.

Without the weight of another's stare,
no one to judge who you choose to meet.
Just breathing the same untroubled air,
if we lived without the need to compete.

V

Her Name was Judy
FREE VERSE

I drove through her last breath
like red lights would absolve me.
She died while I was in motion -
an hour out, maybe less.
I'd stopped at work that morning,
sent emails no one remembers,
like routine could delay the inevitable.
It couldn't.

I still remember the TV was on,
weeks before - the last time
I saw her still breathing.
Westerns, or maybe golf.
She was in the hospital bed
where the recliner used to be,
facing a screen that didn't speak to her.
My father had the remote, focused
on how he would go on without her,
while I resented his self-absorbed control.
I said, okay, I'll see you later,
and left without saying
what I wanted to say.
Everything I meant to say waited too long.

There are no more offhand stories -
no confessions over cigarettes
about barroom apartments and toddler whiskey.
She used to live over the kind of place
you meet a man like my father in.
She played piano by ear.
I don't know how much she knew on guitar.
She never got to show me.

I quit smoking after she died.
Not because I wanted to -
because it felt wrong to keep the ritual
without her beside me.
We'd sit in the garage, cold,
ashtrays full of unsaid things.
I offered more cigarettes
than she would've asked for.
I wonder if I helped kill her.

I fall apart every year on her birthday.
Say I'm fine. I'm not.
Not even close to human.
I carry that day like a blown-out lung.
Every silence is shaped like her.
Every memory cuts.
No one knows what to say
when a mother dies.

I ended up with her afghans,
her loveseat,
her guitar.
The house is empty now –
he died two years later.
But it's not my home,
not anymore.
Just a tomb with closets
for a family I've never met.
Just a timeline I can't walk backwards through.

There are people who tell me to move on,
that grief is a season
with a finish line.
But this isn't winter.
It's marrow-deep.
It's coded.
There's no moving on.
Just moving differently.

She never told me she loved me.
Not once, not that I remember.
And I couldn't say it either.
I meant to.
I really meant to.
It lodged in my throat, a rusted nail.
I told her I'd see her again.
I lied.

The idea of god doesn't help.
Neither do candles, casseroles,
tissue boxes in the shape of angels,
or the quiet way people say
she's in a better place.
No.

The better place was here,
where she was,
until she wasn't.

I am a cathedral of almosts.
A mausoleum of what-ifs.
There are days I don't want
anyone near me,
because they will leave -
the good ones always do.
And I can't survive
another vacancy that deep.

I'm not stronger than this;
I'm not grateful for the time I had.
I'm just here.
With the shape of her
carved into everything I try to hold.
There is no metaphor big enough.
No language sharp enough.

Some holes don't echo.
Some stay quiet -
not empty, just never whole again.
I get through most days
by not touching the edges too much.
By not speaking her name out loud
or in my mind.

There is no closure.
Only the quiet
of living without her
and pretending
it doesn't cost me everything.

Triage
TERZA RIMA

The word came slow, like glass against the vein,
and still I smiled, my voice a steady rope.
I kept her laughing through the undertow of pain.

In every room, I played the part of hope,
the son who wouldn't let the shadows win,
though in the dark, my hands could barely cope.

Her eyes would find me, asking where I'd been,
and I would lie, say I'd been getting rest,
while spackling up the cracks beneath my skin.

You learn to hide the heart inside your chest,
to tend the wounds in places no one sees,
and leave your tears for corners unaddressed.

This is the art of quiet triage - these
are the days where breathing feels like loss,
and cancer's work of holding up disease.

Caterpillar Corpses
TAVERN SONG

I chased the sun through silver fields,
and left my roots in clay.
The seeds I sowed were never sealed,
I threw my time away.

Too late to bloom, the frost now claims,
a shell that never learned its name.

I changed my skin with every turn,
each life a fleeting thread.
But still the wings I longed to earn
lay folded with the dead.

Too late to bloom, the frost now claims,
a shell that never learned its name.

Your breath grows faint, the garden sleeps,
its colors fade to bone.
The path I missed is mine to keep,
but I must walk alone.

Too late to bloom, the frost now claims,
a shell that never learned its name.

I thought there'd be another spring,
another dawn to start.
But time's a blade, and love's the sting
that carves into the heart.

Too late to bloom, the frost now claims,
a shell that never learned its name.

The Screams Stay Inside
PROSE

i.
Hospitals used to mean orange juice cups and coughs in plastic chairs, posters about handwashing, cartoon animals reminding you not to run. I fell from the small log cabin in the park – meant for climbing – and landed sideways, my arm folded like broken cookies at the bottom of my lunch bag, and now we were here, breathing cinnamon and saline while the grownups used nonsense words. The vending machine ate my dollar and gave me pretzels instead of Famous Amos sweets. A nurse smiled and said, "You're brave," and I believed her. I liked the way light pooled under the doorway of every room, like each one contained something quietly glowing. Once, I saw a man wheeled past with a white mesh mask over his face. I assumed it was part of something I didn't need to understand.

ii.
Now the light spills differently - it clings to the floor like something ashamed. We came every day, riding the elevator in silence, my father gripping his folder full of doctor's printouts he no longer read. The brain tumors made her speak in signage - EXIT, CAUTION, ROOM 428. She answered our questions with whatever words she could see, and my sister said maybe it meant she still understood. I tested that theory. My father told me to stop. The radiation required a mask, molded to her face like another layer of skin. She didn't know what it was for. She thought she was being punished. When they bolted her to the table, she fought, then wept, then begged in signage. I couldn't touch her - only watch her face twist on the monitor as the vault swallowed her whole. After, we didn't speak. We just walked the hallway, past someone's balloons, past a child coloring outside the infusion room, past a janitor humming like nothing had happened. But the meshed mask stayed. The mesh they made never left.

iii.
Years later, I returned - not for her, but for myself. Different issue, different hospital, the same awful chairs. The nurses were the same but different, swathed in business and breath. I sat in a waiting room that felt the same, though the floor tiles were now a shade of beige. A man cradled his wife's purse while she disappeared behind double doors, and he looked like he hadn't slept in days. I remembered how hospitals rearrange time - how they compress it into murmurs, thick with waiting warm and low. Faces, wondering and waiting, with the long drag of socks beneath soles that forget how to walk anywhere else. I passed an old wing, and even though the vault room wasn't here, I felt it behind the walls, like a scar hidden under bandages. I

thought of the mesh - how the mask molded to her face, how they locked her in place so carefully, as if she was dangerous. I wondered how many had screamed into that mesh, how many still do. Maybe that's what we're all afraid of - to be seen but not heard, to feel pain no one believes, to lose the language that says I am still here. I stared at my reflection in the metal panel on the wall while waiting, unsure of what I was searching for. But there, there it was - something in my eyes I didn't recognize at first. Then I realized: it was her. And it was me. And it was everyone. A child passed me, holding his arm awkwardly, face pale with pain, glancing to the vending machine, its brightly lit options offering still the same empty comforts.

Washing Machine
RONDEAU

We sat out back, the cycles turned,
two chairs, a lighter, smoke that burned.
The hum was soft, the night was still,
our talk was nothing, yet it filled
the gaps where deeper words were spurned.

I'd call you out, the match you'd spurn,
no flinch, no scold, no line discerned.
Now guilt's a stain I cannot spill,
we sat out back.

I wonder if my asks returned
the debt you paid, the fate you earned.
The washer spins, the years distill,
and in its drum I hear you still -
that smoke, that laugh, the lesson learned.
We sat out back.

Oven Doors
SESTINA

You said it started with your hand,
a slip, a hiss, the kiss of heat.
The kitchen hummed, the oven sang,
a Sunday smell, a dinner's call.
You laughed it off, then rinsed the skin,
and told me not to make a fuss.

I tried to match your calm, no fuss,
but still, I saw you guard that hand.
The water cooled the angry skin,
you wrapped it up to keep the heat.
I didn't know that was the call,
that day the turning of the sang.

The days went on, the wound still sang,
a quiet throb beneath the fuss.
You waved away the doctor's call,
you said it's nothing, it's my hand.
But still it burned with hidden heat,
a warning buried under skin.

And then they found it in your skin,
not in the burn, but where it sang.
A darker ember held the heat,
a different fight, a louder fuss.
I traced the path back to your hand,
to where the story made its call.

I wish I'd missed that ringing call,
or stopped you from that reach, that skin
against the gleam of steel and hand.
But fate had scored the song it sang,
and life will always make its fuss
from something small as kitchen heat.

I hate the taste of oven heat,
the way it hums like some old call.
It makes my heart a restless fuss,
it makes me feel you in my skin.
And every night the same song sang -
all this because you touched the hand.

The heat still steeps beneath my skin.
The call still sings. The song still sang.
All from the fuss of your burned hand.

Fluorescent Lights
PANTOUM

The hum above won't let me sleep.
I count the words I never said.
The hallway air is cold and deep.
I make a list of all I dread.

I count the words I never said,
the birthdays missed, the calls ignored.
I make a list of all I dread,
how grief keeps knocking at the door.

The birthdays missed, the calls ignored,
they pile like coats nobody claims.
How grief keeps knocking at the door,
while nurses pass and call our names.

They pile like coats nobody claims,
reminding me I'm here to stay.
While nurses pass and call our names,
I think of what I'd trade away.

Reminding me I'm here to stay,
the hallway air is cold and deep.
I think of what I'd trade away,
the hum above won't let me sleep.

Confession
TRIVERSEN

I thought there would be time,
more evenings in the kitchen,
you stirring coffee, me finding courage.

The words stayed under my tongue,
too heavy to lift,
too sharp to let drop.

I told you the small things,
weather and neighbors and TV reruns,
when I wanted to hand you my heart.

Now the phone is silent,
your chair stays empty,
and I rehearse a speech for no one.

Every sentence ends
where your breath used to start,
and I am still waiting for you to answer.

What We Left Unsaid
NONET

We learned to keep our hearts behind lips,
to nod instead of what we meant.
The air grew heavy with weight,
words turning to silence.
Hands stayed in own space,
eyes looked away.
Never said.
Never.
Gone.

VI

Medi-nation
BLUES

They say one more pill's gonna fix what's wrong.
Yeah, they say one more pill's gonna fix what's wrong.
Sixteen every morning, and the list's still long.

The bottle caps rattle when I walk the floor.
Yeah, the bottle caps rattle when I walk the floor.
Every step I'm counting what I can't ignore.

The doc shakes his head, says we'll try this too.
Oh, the doc shakes his head, says we'll try this too.
But every cure he sells just makes something new.

I got reds, I got blues, I got whites in rows.
Yeah, I got reds, I got blues, I got whites in rows.
They're the colors of the flag for the life I chose.

The water runs cold as it washes them down.
Yeah, the water runs cold as it washes them down.
I'm afloat in this ocean, but I swear I'll drown.

Can't remember my body without the haze.
No, I can't remember my body without the haze.
It's a medicated march through my numbered days.

They say one more pill's gonna fix what's wrong.
Yeah, they say one more pill's gonna fix what's wrong.
Sixteen every morning, and the list's still long.

Chasing Ambulances
SONG

Neon lights in the midnight rain,
sirens singing in a silver chain.
Every breath is a borrowed flame,
every heartbeat calls my name.

We're not running for the thrill,
we're just learning how to stand still.

Chasing ambulances down the street,
dancing on the edge with heavy feet.
If the end is closer than it seems,
I'll paint it gold inside my dreams.

Faces blur in the rearview glass,
time keeps moving, but we can't pass.
Every fear is a shadow's dance,
every fall is a second chance.

We're not running for the thrill,
we're just learning how to stand still.

Chasing ambulances down the street,
dancing on the edge with heavy feet.
If the end is closer than it seems,
I'll paint it gold inside my dreams.

Every siren's song reminds me
that the road is all we have.
Every flashing light defines me,
every moment's all we grab.

Chasing ambulances down the street,
dancing on the edge with heavy feet.
If the end is closer than it seems,
I'll paint it gold inside my dreams.

December
SONG

Frost on the frame, flame fading low,
another year gone where I don't know.
Counting the cracks in the mirror's face,
time keeps winning this endless race.

December, remember, the snow's still cold,
the fire's still burning but the coals grow old.
I'm closer to nowhere with every day,
but the wind still whispers I should stay.

Candles collapse, wax runs thin,
another year out, another year in.
Shadows stretch long where the sunlight dies,
and I'm still searching for reason's eyes.

December, remember, the snow's still cold,
the fire's still burning but the coals grow old.
I'm closer to nowhere with every day,
but the wind still whispers I should stay.

Silver sky, slow goodbye,
breath turns brittle in the night.
Every tear, every try,
still can't tell me why it's right.

December, remember, the snow's still cold,
the fire's still burning but the coals grow old.
I'm closer to nowhere with every day,
but the wind still whispers I should stay.

The Skill of Skulls
FREE VERSE

The road takes no pity.
It winds through fen and frost,
through markets reeking of hot iron and old blood.
Merchants with coin-slick smiles
sell relics of lives spent poorly.
A cup chipped at the lip.
A blade worn blunt from battles it did not win.
A skull, polished clean,
its jaw hinged open as if still speaking.

I have been such a jaw.
I have spoken to those who would not hear,
shouted into winds that carried my words away,
and bent my knees before gates
that opened for every hand but mine.

They say fortune favors the bold.
But boldness is a purse easily emptied,
and when the last coin is spent,
you are left with the weight of your own name,
and the quiet knowledge
that it will not purchase bread.

So I walked.
I walked until my soles split.
I walked until my shadow learned my gait
and slunk ahead of me like a guide.
I stumbled on stones hidden in the grass.
I bled where thorns kissed the skin raw.
I was mocked by the crow on the fencepost,
by the frost that came too soon,
by the sun that set before the work was done.

Still, I learned the skill of skulls.
How to keep the shape, though the flesh be gone.
How to endure weather,
how to cradle wisdom in the hollow where the eyes once were.

And when I failed -
and I failed -
I gathered my bones and rose again,
creaking like the old trees do
when winter bends them near to breaking.

The road has no pity,
but it remembers the tread of those
who would not turn back.
And I will walk it,
until my own skull sits clean on some merchant's stall,
and my jaw remains open,
still speaking.

Bruised
VERSE

Bruised, but I'm breathing, I'm beating, I'm here,
scars on the skin but the soul's still clear.
They see the mark and they call it defeat,
but I'm still strong, I'm still complete.

Bag's got weight, yeah, I feel that drag,
scrape in the skin where the colors sag.
Picked too quick or I dropped too far,
still got seeds and a beating heart.
Blemish on the side but the core stays clean,
got dents in the flesh but I'm fit for the scene.
Market don't mark me down, no deal,
I'm still worth the bite, I'm still real.

Bruised, but I'm breathing, I'm beating, I'm here,
scars on the skin but the soul's still clear.
They see the mark and they call it defeat,
but I'm still strong, I'm still complete.

Rot takes time, I'm not there yet,
sun still warm where the shadows set.
Peel back layers, you'll see I'm sound,
roots still deep in the dirt I've found.
Storms shook branches, yeah, I swayed,
but the taste stayed true, never frayed.
They'll pass me by for the shine and the gloss,
but the cost of that's a lot colder loss.

Bruised, but I'm breathing, I'm beating, I'm here,
scars on the skin but the soul's still clear.
They see the mark and they call it defeat,
but I'm still strong, I'm still complete.

Don't judge the fruit till you've felt the tree sway,
till you've seen what survives in the break of the day.
Every crack in the shell's where the sunlight leaks,
that's the proof that my core's still sweet.

Bruised, but I'm breathing, I'm beating, I'm here,
scars on the skin but the soul's still clear.
They see the mark and they call it defeat,
but I'm still strong, I'm still complete.

Diagnosis is a Second Skin
SPOKEN WORD FREE VERSE

The doctor...
they gave it a name.
Wrote it down on paper,
like that would make it lighter.
Like knowing the word
would lift the weight.

But it didn't.
The mornings still press flat.
Sheets still cling like police tape.
Coffee cools before I touch it.
The reflection avoids my eyes.

It doesn't wash off.
No matter how many showers.
No matter how many miles I walk,
how many pills line the counter.
It stays -
slimed at the edges of my breath,
threaded through the seams of my sleep.

Some days I forget.
Not because it's gone,
but because I've learned to carry it
the way skin carries discoloration.
It fades,
but it will never vanish.

I walk in it,
work in it,
try to love in it.
It shifts with me,
pulls when I stretch,
splits when I fight.

And every night,
when the lights are low
and the noise is gone,
I feel it settle back over me,
a second skin
that never asked permission
and never learned how to breathe.

Sedation Station
HAIKU

Pills line up in rows,
day drifts under heavy lids,
life waits at the door.

Pieces of Absinthe
TAVERN VERSE

At dawn's pale blush, the glass sings green,
a jewel of the old world, light as breath.
It coils upon the tongue, sweet fennel,
whispering soft the names of forgotten saints.
The table is dressed in crystal and lace,
the hour unhurried, the morning patient.

Sip upon sip, the sun folds higher,
the chatter of streets dim to a hush.
The glass grows lighter, the mind grows warm,
laughter swells like a summer tide.
The world is velvet, eyes half-lidded,
and sorrow drifts far, far from the shore.

But the glass is never sated.
It calls for another, and then other,
until shadows stain the windowpane
and the lace is spotted with spills.
The tongue grows thick, the breath grows sour,
saints' names slur into a stranger's curse.

Night comes heavy, pressing the bones.
The room sways, the floor tilts,
and the glass still waits, green and patient.
No dawn blushes now,
only the hollow bell of waking -
head split, throat ash, hands trembling -
to gather the shards of yester
and to pour again.

Welcome to Room 2C
LYRICAL FREE VERSE

White walls hum with fluorescent ache,
the clock's slow circle cutting the day
into pieces too small to hold.
The bed rails press against my hips,
plastic flowers wilt in the corner
from a nurse who forgot who left them.

No one comes.
The door stays shut,
except for the shuffle of soft shoes,
the rattle of pills in paper cups.
I watch rain stripe the window,
count the drops,
lose track,
start again.

I think of you,
lying in a room like this,
throat marked by the grip of stage-four lung cancer,
eyes speaking where your mouth could not.
I wonder if the walls whispered to you too,
if the hours folded over themselves
like damp sheets.

Here,
time has no taste.
Food comes on plastic trays
and leaves in plastic bags.
The television talks to itself,
I don't answer.

If you were here,
you'd tell me to get up,
but the air weighs too much.
And all I can do
is lie still in 2C,
counting the drops,
and waiting
for someone to remember
I am here.

Analysis Mine
RONDEAU

I sift the shards of days I keep,
their edges worn, their colors deep.
Each fragment tells of where I've been,
of roads unwalked, of might-have-been,
of promises I failed to reap.

Through mirrored glass my truths still creep,
their shadows stretched, their echoes steep.
I hold them close, though frayed and thin,
analysis mine.

And if the past wakes me from sleep,
I mark the hours, I watch them weep.
Each lesson carved into my shin,
a tally made of loss and sin,
while secrets lie in graves I sweep -
analysis mine.

My Body
FREE VERSE

Each step creaks louder,
shifts more beneath me.
The banister sighs
under the weight
of all I haven't said.

December brings forty-five,
but my knees feel older,
my breath catches quicker -
not just from the climb,
but from years spent
holding myself underwater,
afraid to surface,
afraid of who might see me there.

I stand at the bathroom mirror,
towel tight around my waist,
skin pale beneath blue-cream lights.
I trace swollen reminders
of lymphedema's claims -
legs etched with lines
I never asked for,
stories I never wanted to tell,
caked with blood and exposure.

There's no bullet wound
from any war,
no trophy stitches from barroom nights -
just quiet accumulation
of safety,
of caution,
of not speaking up
or stepping out.

My eyes stare back,
dirty green I've never liked -
muddy ponds reflecting
everything I've avoided.
I have been gentle with myself -
perhaps too gentle,
letting fear carve me careful,
until the body in the mirror
became a stranger.

My hands are older now,
valleys of space slipping south
with every passing week, month,
year, regret, failure.
Roots in a ground I never loved,
years passing
like cars I never drove,
opportunities waving
from the rearview mirror,
growing smaller with time.

No friends here.
Family reduced to silence -
birthdays remembered by automated emails,
coupons for meals
I eat alone.

This was never meant to be home.

Sometimes, at night,
I still feel their hands
in shadows at the edge of sleep -
fingerprints embedded
like nails beneath skin.
Family who knew,
who chose silence and comfort
over safety,
over truth.

Over me.

One love, once:
psychopath eyes calm as winter lakes;
kindness worn as costume -
bruises left deeper than flesh.
They took what wasn't given,
discarded me, broken fruit -
yet I stayed,
until they decided
even my brokenness
was too empty to keep.

What kind of broken
isn't even enough
to hold the love
of a monster?

Therapy, now nineteen months deep,
my therapist gentle-voiced,
a man teaching me softly
I am more than hands on skin,
more than my actions and pain,
more than the blackness
pooled behind my chest -
now a dark charcoal,
lightened with tinges of hope.

A safe space: two canvas hammock chairs
I'm too heavy to try,
but maybe someday -
facing an off-white couch
hemmed by the metal tree
and scent of teas.
Four floors, up the sky,
creaking, cracking, elevator slow,
threatening to snap, plummet
into a pile of twisted rebar and dust -
the stairs too much for my body,
the lift too much for my nerve.

Terrified these swollen limbs
might one day fail me,
leave me stranded, stairs impassable,
hopeless and homeless and unseen.

I think of my desk,
large table in lieu of dining.
Manuscripts in my drawer
yellow like tea-stained teeth.
I moved here chasing a paycheck,
not a purpose -
now trapped,
a peace lily forgotten
under a close-curtained windowsill.

But tonight,
in this ordinary reflection,
something trembles -
leaves before rain,
sparks in cold ash -
a quiet ache,
a pull,
almost -

Courage comes slow -
as if asking permission
to believe I might deserve it.

The mirror softens,
the swollen scars, the heavy lines
forming a different kind of map -
roads yet unexplored,
routes away from regret.

What if,
instead of adding more silence,
I mark myself clearly
with proof I have tried?
What if these lines,
deepening along my forehead,
the heavy circles beneath my eyes,
are just first drafts?

What if this body,
so long held prisoner,
could become
a story written
in muscle, in voice,
in defiant, living ink?
My heartbeat, thundering so loudly,
I can feel it without touching.
Breath caught sharp and sudden -
panic attacks like memories,
severed hands grabbing from shadows,
without warning.

I trace flesh on my forearm
where fingers once bruised,
held me still,
stole safety I never reclaimed.
A stomach wound slow to heal -
open still, like questions unanswered,
or forgiveness not yet offered.

Tomorrow,
I might step outside -
feel sunlight on my skin,
meet the gaze of strangers
without flinching.

Maybe I will write,
fingers trembling on keys,
unafraid of rejection
that cannot leave
more emptiness
than silence already carved.

I hover fingers along
the marks I carry,
these scars of flesh,
scars of silence,
memories I never chose.
Each line -
an opportunity,
a story,
a breath,
a choice.

Maybe I'll make new scars -
small cuts earned
by speaking,
by reaching out,
by stepping forward
instead of standing still.

I am not young,
but tonight,
for the first time in years,
I am not yet old.
I am breathing,
I am here -
in my body,
flawed, uncertain,
but mine.

I meet my own eyes
in the glass,
daring to recognize myself
as someone
worth wanting.

I am breathing,
I am here -
in my body,
scarred, imperfect,
but perhaps

still capable of catching
what I stopped chasing
long ago.

Tonight, now,
in this fragile moment
tenuous and fleeting,
stitched with hope and quiet,
I recognize myself for a moment:
someone worth choosing.

For the first time,
that feels enough.

VII

Jack and Me
VILLANELLE

Jack waits for me in the dark.
His breath smells the same as my father's did.
I drink to forget what I know.

The bottle's a flare and a spark,
a promise I swore I'd forbid.
Jack waits for me in the dark.

I watch as the evening grows stark,
as memory lifts off the lid.
I drink to forget what I know.

He died with his shame as a mark,
I swore I would not do as he did.
Jack waits for me in the dark.

The taste is both bitter and stark,
and sweet like the lie of a kid.
I drink to forget what I know.

Our bloodline runs deep with Maker's Mark;
it swallows the best that we hid.
Jack waits for me in the dark.
I drink to forget what I know.

Hey
FREE VERSE

i don't have the right words.
i don't think there are any.

but here i am, anyway -
not because i know what to say,
but because silence feels too much
like doing nothing.

i know you're not the type
to want people fussing.

you're probably still
making the phone calls,
checking in on your mom,
shoveling the parts of grief
that pile up in quiet corners.

maybe telling yourself
you're fine enough
for now.

but losing a parent -
even when the relationship
is solid, or strained,
or quietly in-between -
is like someone rearranged the floor
and forgot to tell you.

you keep walking
like the path is still there,
until your footing says otherwise.

i didn't know him.

i won't pretend i did.

but i know this:
when someone who shaped you
leaves the room for good,
the echo of their absence
sticks to the walls
long after the shock wears off.

and there's no handbook
for how you're supposed to
clean around it.

this isn't meant to fix anything.

it can't.

it's not enough.

i know that.

i just want to give you
one moment
where someone else
carries a sliver of it
with you.

so this is me,
trying to say:
it's okay if it hits you sideways.

if you feel more
than you let on.

if you keep your voice steady
but your hands shake
when you remember
a story he used to tell,
even if it was the same one
every damn time.

i don't have advice.

i don't have answers.

but if you ever need to not be strong
for a little while,
that's okay.

i promise.

and if these lines
can do nothing else,
let them be
a quiet chair

beside yours
while the world
keeps asking you
to move.

Exuviae External
FREE VERSE

I have worn so many skins
I can't remember which one was mine.

Each chrysalis feels final,
sealed in silk and the promise
of becoming.
Inside,
I rehearse my wings.

But the day I break open,
the air is wrong.
The proboscis curls back on itself,
the scales fall from my wings
before they dry.

I crawl again,
wrong shape for the world
and too heavy for the sky.

They tell me I should be grateful
for the metamorphosis.
They do not see
the husks piled behind me,
bodies I've outgrown
without ever getting to live in them.

Neurodivergence
is the molt you can't control.
The pupa never rests long enough
to let the mind
catch up with the body.

Every time I figure myself out,
I leave another exuviae
clinging to a branch I'll never revisit,
its hollow eyes watching
as I stumble toward
the next version of myself
I will not get to keep.

Decomposition of a Song
FOLK SONG

(Folk Ballad in G Major, 4/4 time)

G C G D
We marched in step, the drums kept time,
G C D
Banners waved, the horns would shine.
Em C G D
I dreamed my place was at the head,
C G D G
To lift the call the music said.

G C G D
The day had come, the field was mine,
G C D
The notes were clear, the lines in line.
Em C G D
The score was set, my hands held high,
C G D G
Until his pen rewrote the lie.

G C G D
"He'll be a senior, his folks are near,
G C D
The choice is plain, the path is clear."
Em C G D
They tore the stripes I'd yet to wear,
C G D G
And left me standing, stripped and bare.

(slight drop in tempo)
G C G D
Next year I tried the game again,
G C D
The horn still bright, the beat still then.
Em C G D
But politics still called the tune,
C G D G
And I was silenced far too soon.

Em C G D
The drumbeat stumbled, horns grew thin,
Em C D
The march gave way to weight within.
Em C G D
The refrain I'd sung fell out of key,
Am C G G
And none of them would sing with me.

Em C G
Music turns to ash in my mouth.
D
Rhythm walks - away.
Em C
I don't…
G D G
I don't trust the hands on the score.

(no chord)
no band
no banner
no sound
nothing promised is true.

Muscle Words
FREE VERSE

You messaged me again.

I've fallen asleep writing replies I never send.
Whole conversations unravel behind my fingers
like thread that forgot what it was holding
together.
I answer your messages in my head -
not just yours -
everyone's.
A hundred times a day.
And none of them ever feel safe enough to send.

I know you think I'm distant.
That I'm not trying.
That I gave up.
You're not wrong.
But you're not right either.
Trying looks different when your ribs still remember
what it's like to be kicked.

I don't know how to say I miss people
without feeling like I'm setting a trap -
like if I say it too loud,
they'll hear the emptiness
and decide to leave anyway.
Every silence becomes the proof.

The dead part of me -
what never grew back
after everything that happened -
doesn't believe love means stay.
It believes stay means wait -
wait until the betrayal.
Wait until the twist.
Wait until you're no longer worth the effort.

It's not pessimism.
It's muscle memory.

I've watched too many smiles curdle
into weapons.
Watched I care turn into I can't do this anymore.
Watched the glass teeter on the edge

and chosen to walk away
just so I didn't have to hear it shatter.

You say you won't hurt me.
But so did everyone else.

I know I sound melodramatic.
Exhausting.
Impossible to reassure.
But when you've been burned
by the people who were supposed to protect you,
your skin doesn't forget the pattern.
It recoils in a cold room.

There are days I can't speak.
Not because I don't want to,
but because I've convinced myself
that silence will hurt less
than whatever your reply might be.
Or worse - no reply at all.

You ask how I'm doing.
I want to ask why.
Why you're asking.
Why now.
Why it matters.

I don't believe you when you say you care.
Not because you're lying -
because I can't afford to be wrong again.
Not after what it took
to survive the last time.

Somewhere in me,
I am still thirteen and screaming,
and no one is coming.
I am still twenty and hollowed out,
a body that kept breathing
after its spirit was carved out clean.

I am a stopped clock.
Everyone else keeps moving
and I stay frozen,
just ticking.
Just echoing.

I've been in mourning for so long,
I wouldn't know who I am without it.
I think that's the worst part -
not the pain,
but how familiar it's become.

Now it's rot in the foundation,
and everyone who gets too close
eventually smells the truth.

And when the whole world teaches you
that connection is a trap,
you learn to chew through your own leg
before trusting a hand that feeds.
And even when the cage door stays open,
you don't leave -
you just learn
how to live without moving.

But maybe tomorrow,
I'll try to write you back.
Again.

Capricornicopia
RHYMING QUATRAINS

I climb the hill the stars have drawn,
Each stone a weight I walk upon.
The summit hides behind the cloud,
The wind is sharp, the sky is loud.

I plan the path, I mark each mile,
I wear my patience like a trial.
The rules I follow twist and break,
Yet still I bend, yet still I ache.

The world feels carved for lighter feet,
Not ones that drag through ice and sleet.
I watch the doors swing shut and lock,
I count the hours and hear them knock.

My hands build walls, then tear them down,
I wear a mask, I wear a crown.
A worker's spine, a dreamer's eye,
A stubborn Will that will not die.

And yet I stand outside the gate,
With all I've earned, and all I wait.
Capricorn heart, too hard, too slow,
Still chasing where I'll never go.

The Dying Flowers
FREE VERSE

The clock does not stop
when your chest is caving in.
The sun still rises,
its light spilling across cracked sidewalks,
touching the same faces
that never knew your name.

In the yard,
the grass bends under its own green weight.
Weeds push through soil
as if they've never heard of grief.
A bee lands on a petal
already browning at the edges,
drinks from it anyway.

You tell yourself the garden is ruined.
Too many blooms have curled inward,
too many stems have snapped under rain.
But still, something stirs in the dirt.
An ant crawls across a fallen leaf.
The wind carries pollen
to places you'll never see.

You've buried more than you've planted.
You've let dreams rot
in the dark,
covered them with years of excuses,
watched them become compost
for someone else's ambition.

And yet,
the green keeps creeping forward,
tendrils wrapping around rusted fences,
vines swallowing the corners of the shed.
The world is not waiting for you
to be ready.

Some days you kneel in the soil,
pulling weeds with hands that shake,
trying to control what will not be controlled.
Other days, you let them grow wild
because they're the only things
that seem to want to live.

Life doesn't pause for pain.
It doesn't step aside
to let you catch your breath.
It marches,
steady as root growth beneath the frost.

The flowers die.
The flowers always die.
But still, they come back,
fragile and stubborn,
as if they've never learned
what winter means.

God of Screams
BLANK VERSE

Within these bones a prison cell is wrought,
its walls unyielding, forged of years and ash.
My voice, a tide that breaks yet leaves no mark,
is swallowed whole by air too thick to breathe.

I walk through halls of memory, unlit,
where shadows clutch the remnants of my name.
Each step resounds like iron on the stone,
yet none will turn to hear the sound I make.

Once I had thought the world was shaped for me,
a place where blood and toil would earn me grace.
But now the wind moves past without my scent,
and even gods have turned their gaze away.

I am the keeper of a hollow shrine,
its altar bare, save for the echo's crown.
No supplicant will kneel, no prayer will rise,
save those I whisper to my own deaf ears.

If I should break, my soul will be quiet,
a silent rift the earth will not record.
For I am he who rules the wasted realm,
and reigns alone, the God of Screams, unheard.

Tuesday Mornings
ANACREONTIC VERSE

Calendar pings,
agenda slides,
screens glow cold,
eyes red-tired.

Coaching ticket,
wrong assignee,
Adobe won't load,
still they see me.

Stand-up's late,
chat scrolls on,
mute stays off,
my words are gone.

KPI breath,
targets spin,
another deck,
another win.

Email says yes,
meeting says no,
deadlines circle,
nothing to show.

Lunch in six,
calls in four,
log the task,
still there's more.

Quarterly close,
numbers climb,
performance met,
not worth the time.

To: The Devil
FREE VERSE

take it
take all of it
not
the paper flaking in the wind
the sheets of my soul

take
this heat
this rising
take this claw
of tooth and glass
take these lips
i don't need them

rip it out
the voice that still whispers nothing
that slams with smells and sinew
rip off the flesh
from my blood and bone
make it hurt so much
i don't remember

show me where
the unanswered go
why
with prayers and pleads
to closed ears and eyes
show me
a true hate I can't burn away
but why
i want you to show me
what real hatred feels like
so this burden is easier to carry

make me feel like myself
when I can't feel anything anymore
make me scream my own name
when I can't see anything anymore

i don't deserve it
i didn't deserve it
why did i deserve it
just let it all burn

The Silence of Gods
HEROIC COUPLETS

I knelt on stones that split my knees,
to beg the wind, to move the seas.
Yet all was still, the air was cold,
and no hand reached, no comfort told.

The stars above would watch, but lie,
their silver gaze a vacant eye.
They marked my wounds, my crooked frame,
yet never once they spoke my name.

I burned the tithes I could not spare,
to smoke the heavens, choke the air.
But clouds held fast, no sign was shown,
their thrones unmoved, their faces stone.

They set my birth in shadow's keep,
where wolves took meat and left me sleep.
Where mouths would smile with sharpened teeth,
and silence crushed the breath beneath.

They gave me hands that ache for art,
but bound them tight before the start.
They filled my head with restless fire,
then drowned my tongue in mud and mire.

They shaped my face from jagged clay,
then cursed the sun to hide the day.
They crowned my heart with longing's weight,
then sealed it fast with rusted gate.

So tell me why your altars stand,
with gilded cup in gilded hand.
Why hymns are sung to deafened ears,
while I am ground by all my years.

If gods there be, they feast on cries,
they drink the salt from mortal eyes.
And should they kneel before me now,
I'd break their crowns, I'd teach them how.

For what are gods who turn away,
and let the lamb be led astray?
No more my knee, no more my prayer,
I owe them naught. Let them despair.

Please Stop Asking if I'm Okay
FREE VERSE

Please stop asking if I'm okay.
The question feels like a spotlight,
burning through the paint I've smeared on my face
to make it look like I belong in this room.

I wake up every morning
and drag my skin into shape
that passes for human.
I answer emails. I laugh at the right time.
I stand in the kitchen
and pretend to want dinner.

But there's a jutting in my chest,
and every breath drives it deeper.
The truth is a wound I cannot show you;
It will make you look away.

Please stop asking if I'm okay.
Because I will lie.
Because you will believe me.
Because we will both nod and change the subject,
and I will hate how easy it was.

There are days
I am so far from myself
I could wave from across the street
and not recognize the hand.
There are days
I stand in the shower,
water hammocking my back,
just to feel something that doesn't ask questions.

I am not okay.
I am a thorn pulled thin,
fraying at every end.
I am a locked room
with the lights off.

Please stop asking if I'm okay.
It feels like you want me to say yes.
It feels like you'd leave if I said no.

So I will smile
and hold your gaze
and tell you I'm fine.
And you will nod,
and we will both walk away,
and I will keep the truth
where no one can see it.

Body in the Back
HAIKU

Body in the back,
Dreams wrapped in cellophane tears.
I go on alone.

The Teeth in the Light
TRIOLET

I bite the air, I take my place,
though years have slipped between my hands.
The fight is carved into my face,
I bite the air, I take my place.

If I should fall, I'll bear the trace,
my name still burning in the sands.
I bite the air, I take my place,
though years have slipped between my hands.

VIII

Freezer
BALLAD

Cold hum in the kitchen,
white door like a wall.
Hands pressed to the metal,
and there's no one to call.
Snow in my chest,
ice is in my veins.
Dreams are turning brittle,
heart too heavy with chains.

Silence so sharp
it can cut me in two,
and I'm staring straight through
the world I once knew.

Freezer, hold me,
keep me from burning.
Lock all the doors
on the life I've been spurning.
If the night takes me,
don't let it deceive -
I'm frozen in place,
and I can't seem to leave.

Shadows in the doorway,
time drips from the clock.
My breath is a ghost,
but I still hear it knock.
Light through the curtains,
beams are thin as a thread,
can't warm this frosting over
or the words inside my head.

Silence so loud
that it deafens the pain,
and I'm calling your name,
but it's lost in the chain.

Freezer, hold me,
keep me from burning.
Lock all the doors
on the life I've been spurning.
If the night takes me,

don't let it deceive -
I'm frozen in place,
and I can't seem to leave.

If there's heat in the world,
I've forgotten its sound.
I'm a heart that won't beat,
I'm a soul that's been bound.
But the frost has a mercy,
a mercy so deep,
that it whispers to me slowly,
and it lulls me to sleep.

Freezer, hold me,
keep me from burning.
Lock all the doors
on the life I've been spurning.
If the night takes me,
don't let it deceive -
I'm frozen in place,
and I can't seem to leave.

Cold hum in the kitchen,
white door like a wall.
The frost is the only
friend left to call.

A Thousand Ways to Die
TAVERN SONG

Through halls of stone and shadowed keep,
where moonlight falls but cannot sleep,
I walk the boards that groan and bend,
each step a prayer that meets no end.
The wind it wails of nameless graves,
the sea it sings to hollow caves,
and in my chest the echoes cry,
a thousand ways, a thousand ways to die.

So raise your cups, the night grows cold,
drink to stories never told.
The crown of death is carved in bone,
and no one leaves this hall alone.

By noose of hemp, by blade of rust,
by whispered oath betrayed of trust,
by frost that bites through skin and soul,
by flames that take, yet leave a hole.
Each day a tally burned in pine,
each night a draught of bitter wine,
yet still I breathe, yet still I lie,
a thousand ways, a thousand ways to die.

So raise your cups, the night grows cold,
drink to stories never told.
The crown of death is carved in bone,
and no one leaves this hall alone.

Through battles lost, through fires waned,
through debts unpaid, through blood retained,
I see the gates where mourners tread,
I smell the rot, the stench of dead.
The stars above refuse their light,
the blackened sky devours sight,
though I've no will, I still defy,
a thousand ways, a thousand ways to die.

So raise your cups, the night grows cold,
drink to stories never told.
The crown of death is carved in bone,
and no one leaves this hall alone.

At last I stand where rivers part,
with ash for breath, with stone for heart,
the voices call, they know my name,
they ask me now to play the game.
No dawn will come, no sun will rise,
the glass is full of hollow lies,
this time I drink, this time I try,
a thousand ways, a thousand ways to die.

So raise your cups, the night grows cold,
drink to stories never told.
The crown of death is carved in bone,
and no one leaves this hall alone.

Why Did the Sky Forget Me
VILLANELLE

Why did the sky forget my face?
I prayed to clouds, they turned away.
No heaven left, no holy place.

The sun burned cold in empty space,
the night refused the break of day.
Why did the sky forget my face?

I begged for light, for some small trace,
but wind and rain would not obey.
No heaven left, no holy place.

Each whispered plea met with disgrace,
each star fell blind to what I say.
Why did the sky forget my face?

If God won't grant a lost embrace,
then why should I be made to stay?
No heaven left, no holy place.

I'll drift beyond this mortal chase,
and let the dark become my clay.
Why did the sky forget my face?
No heaven left, no holy place.

My Eulogy
SONG

Would they dress me in white like I'd never been stained,
Would they tell all the lies so they're spared from the pain,
Would they laugh in the kitchen while my body lies still,
Pass the plates, pass the blame,
Pass the ghost they can't kill.

Would they talk about strength when they meant I endured,
Would they swear they were there when my vision was blurred,
Would they whisper my name like it still had a home,
Or would it sound like a word
They'd forgotten to own.

If I could hear my eulogy,
Would I still stay?
Would I still breathe?
If I could hear the way they pray,
Would I believe in anything?
Would the cosmos even keep my name,
Or would it bleed into the black,
And be the same…
As never being here at all.

Would they open their mouths and confess what they've done,
Or seal it in silence until the day's gone,
Would they cry for my ghost or the weight they now bear,
Would they look at the ground,
Would they even care?

Would the last time they say me be the day that I go,
Would they bury the truth in the frost and the snow,
Would they speak like the sky ever noticed my face,
Or admit that for years
It forgot this place.

If I could hear my eulogy,
Would I still stay?
Would I still breathe?
If I could hear the way they pray,
Would I believe in anything?
Would the cosmos even keep my name,
Or would it bleed into the black,
And be the same…
As never being here at all.

Say my name (my name, my name),
But don't you lie (lie, lie).
Show my wounds (my wounds, my scars),
Don't paint me kind (I'm not bli-i-ind).
Tell the whole wide world
How you let me fall,
Tell the truth…
Or say nothing… nothing, nothing…
nothing at all.

If I could hear my eulogy,
Would I still stay?
Would I still breathe?
If I could hear the way they pray,
Would I believe in anything?
Would the cosmos even keep my name,
Or would it bleed into the black,
And be the same…
As never being here at all.

Would the last time you say me…
Be the last time I'm known…
And would I want to hear it…
If I'm already gone…

Don't Count the Pills
RHYTHM VERSE

I keep the bottle on the nightstand, ticking like a bomb,
Every cap twist echoes, "Kid, you won't last long."
It's a rattlesnake prayer in a plastic skin,
Every dose is a ghost that I'm swallowing in.
Doctor says compliance, I call it decay,
Like feeding myself in reverse every day.
Sixteen little soldiers in a line for my throat,
March it in, tear it down, leave nothing back but a note.

Don't count the pills -
They're just numbers on the wall.
Don't count the pills -
You'll forget you had them all.

They're just little graves in my bloodstream,
Little white lies in a red sea dream.
I can't tell if I'm healing or killing,
If I'm breathing, or willing to fall.
Don't count the pills at all.

Call it chemistry, call it mercy, call it sin,
Call it whatever makes the mirror let me in.
Every swallow feels hollow but I'm painted in jack,
If I spit them all out, will I still come back?
Every morning is a meeting with the same parade,
Tiny faces, no names, just a number engraved.
I'm a math problem dying on a bathroom floor,
Subtract one more, subtract one more.

Don't count the pills -
You won't like what you find.
Don't count the pills -
Just leave the math behind.

They're just little graves in my bloodstream,
Little white lies in a red sea dream.
I can't tell if I'm healing or killing,
If I'm breathing, or willing to fall.
Don't count the pills at all.

It's not the milligrams, it's the minutes they steal,
Not the label on the bottle, it's the way it makes you kneel.
I've been praying to a pharmacy that never heard a word,
Guess salvation's just a side effect you never really earn.

They're just little graves in my bloodstream,
Little white lies in a red sea dream.
I can't tell if I'm healing or killing,
If I'm breathing, or willing to fall…

…don't count the pills at all.

Anatomy of an Echo
SONG

I keep my trophies in a box I can't unlock,
Every victory's a shadow, every step turns to chalk.
I've been climbing up the ladders that collapse when I rise,
Every summit disappears when I open my eyes.

I've been tracing all my failures like they're lines in my skin,
Every scar another story I was supposed to win.
But the walls keep closing in with a whisper, I know -
Every voice in my head is just an echo.

What's the anatomy of an echo?
It's the bones of the words I can't let go.
Every "almost," every "never," every time that I fall,
Rings out in the dark like it's my soul come to call.
What's the anatomy of an echo?
It's the ghost that I've carried all along.

I've tried painting over memories in colors I dreamed,
But the canvas bleeds through with the truths I've screamed.
Every hand that reached out just let me slip,
Every promise was a thorn with a poisoned tip.

I've been running toward the light that was only a flame,
Every flicker just a trick, every loss wears my name.
And the mirrors in my chest, they just show me below,
Every beat of my heart - it's an echo.

What's the anatomy of an echo?
It's the bones of the words I can't let go.
Every "almost," every "never," every time that I fall,
Rings out in the dark like it's my soul come to call.
What's the anatomy of an echo?
It's the ghost that I've carried all along.

Break me, shape me, I still remain,
Shatter my name, but the sound's the same.
Every wound just teaches me to bleed in tune,
Every song I write is a funeral room.

What's the anatomy of an echo (echo, echo, echo)?
It's the bones of the words I can't let go (let it a-a-all go).
Every "almost," every "never," every time that I fall,
Rings out in the dark like it's my soul come to call.
What's the anatomy of an echo (echo, echo, echo)?
It's the ghost that I've carried all along -
And it's singing my song.

I keep my trophies in a box I can't unlock…
Every victory's a shadow… every step turns…

Unstitch me a Butterfly
FREE VERSE

Rip the wings from my shadow.
Pull the thread until my seams collapse -
until every color I've carried leaks into the gutter.

I've been trying to bleach the past out of my blood,
but the stains grow roots,
and the roots choke my veins.

They tell me time is the tailor.
They tell me sleep will slip me whole.
But the nightmares sew me back to the same corpse
every night,
their needle a memory,
their thread made of screams.

I burn my own hands to feel something else.
I drown clocks in rusted paint
just to stop their mouths from ticking my name.

Every exit I take
is a hallway that bends back into my own skull.
Every lock I break
is just another room in this endless autopsy.

I keep asking -
what's the point of breaking free
if the cage remembers you better than you remember yourself?

Unstitch me,
tear me down to paper and air,
scatter me like dead confetti
across the asphalt glaze.

Let the wind forget my shape,
let the rain wash the wings from my back.
Let the past starve without my pulse to feed it,
because I am tired of being sewn
to the ghosts
that call themselves my dreams.

Bloodied Intake
BLANK VERSE

Each handshake feels like sand against my teeth.
The smiles are barbed; the laughter has a cost.
They ask for trust and trade it in for spite,
then sell my name for favors I don't want.

I've learned to keep my gaze just past their eyes,
where nothing's warm enough to pull me in.
The air smells like a copper-biting rain,
and every word tastes like it's been rehearsed.

Each time I think I've found a place to stand,
the floor becomes a mouth that swallows me.
And still I crawl back up, with bones still loud,
my hands a hold of bruises I can't hide.

I'm walking closer to the open edge -
each step a friend who never meant the word.
And maybe that's the only mercy left,
to reach the end already stripped of hope.

If there's a gate, I'll walk through dripping red.
If there's a light, I'll turn my face away.
The bloodied intake is the only truth,
and I am done pretending I'm still whole.

Adulate and Undulate
PANTOUM

the tide applauds my sinking in
it crowns my head with shit and stone
I breathe the salt as if it's skin
and call the undertow my home

it crowns my head with shit and stone
while whispering I've always been
and call the undertow my home
because it feels like discipline

while whispering I've always been
it smooths my bones with patient grace
because it feels like discipline
to never leave this brined embrace

it smooths my bones with patient grace
I breathe the salt as if it's skin
to never leave this brined embrace
the tide applauds my sinking in

Dead Before Goodbye
SONG VERSE

I stalled in the hallway,
hands on the frame, heart on the floor.
Phone said, "Come now, it's time,"
but my feet just froze at the door.
Couldn't face the machines,
couldn't face the way her breathing broke.
An hour too late -
and all I had left was the mask they bolted on her skull.

Thirty minutes too long with him.
I sat in the car, watching the clock,
pretending I could turn back
if I never started forward.
When I walked in,
he was already a sheet and a tag.
And I smiled like I was still alive,
but I was rotting from the inside out.

I see them every night -
the radiation mask, the straps,
the gurney rolling slow through a hallway
that never ends.
Every shadow wears their faces.
Every dream ends in the same cold room.
And I wake up
still late.

I tell myself I had reasons -
fear is a weapon, and I loaded it on myself.
But the truth is,
I just couldn't look Death in the eye.
So I gave it to both of them.
Signed my name in silence.
I didn't say goodbye.
I didn't get to say goodbye.

And I will die before I make it right.
And they will haunt me until the day
I am dead before goodbye.

My Chemical Prayer
ROCK VERSE

Pill bottle choir on the nightstand hums -
plastic rosaries rattling in the dark.
The label is scripture,
the dosage a psalm I can't forget.
One for the panic,
one for the ache,
two for the days I can't lift my head,
three just to make it through someone asking "How are you?"

They tell me to "take what you need"
like it's a mercy, not a mandate.
Like living's just an equation,
and my soul's a math problem
solved in milligrams and meal schedules.
But the truth?
I'm not healing.
I'm surviving at pharmaceutical gunpoint.
A hostage to the half-life,
chained to a pill case like it's my coffin hinge.

And God? If you're real, if you're listening,
this isn't a prayer -
it's a dare.
Show me a miracle without a prescription pad.
Show me a sunrise I don't have to swallow whole.

Every morning I baptize my throat
in chalk dust and bitterness.
This is my communion,
body of patient, blood of regret.
Side effects may include -
but hell, I've stopped reading them.
Don't need to know the thousand ways
these little soldiers could betray me -
when I'm the one deploying them.

Some nights I dream I could quit,
walk away from the pharmacy altar,
let my body sing its own song
even if it ends in silence.
But morning always wins -

and I kneel again before the blister pack,
tongue open,
eyes closed.

Because if I stop -
the walls start whispering,
the shadows sharpen,
the floor becomes an ocean
that pulls me under and under and under.
So I take them.
Every damn day.
My little chemical prayers,
lined up like bullets -
and I fire them into my bloodstream
hoping one of them will hit the part of me
that still wants to live.

Amen.
And again, and again…
…tomorrow.

IX

The Empty Chair
SONG VERSE

I pull you closer in my mind,
though you are nowhere near,
A silhouette in faded light,
the ghost I wish was here.
I tell the wood what flesh once heard,
but you are only air,
A thousand things I never spoke
now spill into the chair.

I needed you to guard my name,
to hold my shaking hand,
To keep the dark from seeping in
like flood across the sand.
But every time the storm broke loose,
you closed and turned away -
And still I loved you in the night,
with nothing left to say.

The empty chair -
It hears me cry, it holds my stare.
The words I saved, the pain I bare,
Are pouring out to no one there.
You were the best I'd ever known,
And still, you left me all alone -
I forgive you, though it's not fair…
So I speak to the empty chair.

I wish you'd been a better shield,
I wish you'd yearned to stay,
To see the bruises on my soul
and never look away.
I wanted you to be my home,
a fortress and a flame,
Instead, I learned the bitter truth -
protection wears your name.

And yet I kept you on the throne
inside my breaking chest,
Because a flawed and fragile queen
was still my safest bet.
I begged for more than scraps of love,

for warmth beneath the glare,
But all my pleas just found their grave
inside the empty chair.

The empty chair -
It hears me cry, it holds my stare.
The words I saved, the pain I bare,
Are pouring out to no one there.
You were the best I'd ever known,
And still, you left me all alone -
I forgive you, though it's not fair…
So I speak to the empty chair.

If I could break this wood to splinters,
I'd burn the lies and all the winters.
If I could tear your ghost apart,
I'd stitch the pieces to my heart.
But grief's a lock, and I'm the key—
And rage won't set the captives free.
So I keep talking, just to dare
The silence in the empty chair.

The empty chair -
It hears me cry, it holds my stare.
The words I saved, the pain I bare,
Are pouring out to no one there.
You were the best I'd ever known,
And still, you left me all alone -
I forgive you, though it's not fair…
So I speak to the empty chair.

And when my voice is gone, I swear…
You'll still be there.
The empty chair.

Elegy for Everyone
HAIKU

Grief blooms in all hearts,
but my shadow blinds my eyes;
your tears fall unseen.

What Color is This?
RHYME ROYAL

I point to red, but it is not the flame -
it's rust, it's blood, it's endings dressed in fire.
You call it anger, but it's not the same;
it's bone and ash and longing's slow expire.
I want to name it grief, yet grief's entire
is wrapped in shades that burn and bruise and freeze -
no single word could name a shade like these.

The blue you show me isn't ocean's breath,
it's hospital sheets and the hum of the light,
a cold that keeps you waiting on a death,
a sky that shuts its eyelids to the night.
You call it sadness, but it's not so white -
it's shadows trapped in ice, it's frost on skin,
it's every silence I've been locked within.

And yellow - god, that yellow's wrong as well;
you say it's joy, but joy would never ache.
This shade is teeth beneath a wedding bell,
a smile rehearsed so real it starts to break.
It's sunlit glass that cuts for beauty's sake,
a field of gold that hides the buried bone,
a brightness taught to shine when left alone.

So what color is this? The wheel won't say.
It wants one truth; I live in layered hue.
My tongue holds all the words, but they decay,
and when I hand them over, they aren't true.
The wheel shows simple things I cannot do.
For what I feel is more than colors give -
a palette only pain can let me live.

Remember Wrong
BALLAD

You're brain scribbling while I spill my scene,
hands twitching in time with my halting voice.
I slit up the gaps where the truth has been,
but doubt is a devil who leaves no choice.
The memory flickers, a rusted noise,
a film that skips frames in the reel too long.
Your face stays still, but my gut destroys -
what if I'll ever remember wrong?

I measure each word like a guillotine,
count seconds between when you blink and poise.
Did I say last week what I think I mean,
or have I become just my own ploy?
The lies they accused me of still employ
a chorus that hums in a cursed old song -
and I fear you'll file me as fraud's envoy,
what if I ever remember wrong?

The truth's not a straight line, but it twists obscene,
a Möbius strip in a paper toy.
I'm stuck in the snarl of the in-between,
a hero who fumbles their own convoy.
I'd rather be crushed than be your decoy,
another ghost shuffled in shame's red thong.
But fear's the refrain I can't yet destroy -
what if I somehow remember wrong?

So if I collapse in the words I deploy,
will you still believe that I might belong?
Or will you just hear me like static's coy -
if I ever remember wrong?

The Language of Ceilings
HAIKU

eyes fix on ceiling -
to speak is to stain your soul,
so I drown in shame.

Wednesday Was a Very Bad Day
SONG

I scroll through the shadows, your name in the glow,
Hunting for daggers I'm sure you will throw.
A silence too sudden, a wall in my way,
The glitch of a ghost in the wires today.

Each absence a trigger, each void is a blade,
Cutting through trust that we never made.
I brace for the drop, for the cracks to appear,
For proof of the hate that I've always feared.

It's my fault, it's my shame,
Every wound wears my name.
When I open the door, I choke on the air,
I reach for your hands but find nothing there.

The past is a cage with its locks in my skin,
Every betrayal still burns from deeper within.
A hug is a fracture, a crack in the wall,
One inch of reaching, the risk of a fall.

Your kindness a mirror I can't bear to face,
I search for the sinew, the flaw, the disgrace.
If any moment can shatter, then all of them will,
And the voice in my head whispers, better to kill.

It's my fault, it's my shame,
Every wound wears my name.
When I open the door, I choke on the air,
I reach for your hands but find nothing there.

Love is the curse word that burns every tongue,
A song from the grave that was written too young.
The ghosts in my marrow, the weight in my breath,
Have sung me to sleep with the sound of my death.

It's my fault, it's my shame,
Every wound wears my name.
When I open the door, I choke on the air,
I reach for your hands but find nothing there.

Naming Monsters
TERCET RHYTHM

First, you mouth the name,
the syllables trembling in the air
like glass about to fall.

Then, you let it grow teeth -
see the face you've avoided for years,
map its shadow on the wall.

You speak until the sound
no longer tastes of copper and bile,
until breath stops breaking in your chest.

You strip the monster bare,
learn its gait, its gaze, its gait again -
each loop a lash against its power.

Then comes the taming -
rope of routine around its throat,
pulling until the thrash slows.

Then comes the maiming -
blade of healing in your steady hand,
the wound deep enough to make it stumble.

But you never kill it.
You keep it in a locked room inside you,
a reminder you reclaimed the hunt.

Repair and Contrast
MIRROR

I walk through bright rooms with steady feet,
coffee cooling beside an open window,
faces smiling at me without suspicion,
my voice measured, clear,
my hands unshaken.
I joke about the weather.
I answer messages in time.
I laugh without flinching.

But inside, the glass is still broken -
shards shifting under every coffee steep,
faces that once turned away,
a voice that learned to whisper,
hands that remember restraint,
jokes that were shields,
messages that went unanswered,
laughter that bled slaughter.

Camaros and Caramel
LYRICAL VERSE

Car windows cracked, cold wind cut too clean,
caramel coffee in a cup with cream.
Crank up the cassettes till the dashboard shakes,
countdown clocks on the choices we make.
Could've chased coasts where the breakers bend,
but I clung to chrome like it might not end -
corner-store sugar and streetlight gold,
dreams half-priced in the lies we sold.

Gas-station gum, that grit on my tongue,
gear-shift grins when the night was young.
Gravel-lot laughs and the glow from the sign,
green lights dying before we'd align.
Gave up the gamble for a guaranteed stall,
gave in to gears and the guardrail's call -
greased-up hands in a hometown cage,
writing my name on the same old page.

Now caramel melts in a bitter swirl,
Camaros fade in a flicker-blur whirl.
Could've been more than a mile-long loop,
but I stayed strapped to the same old stoop.
Clock keeps clicking, I can't rewind -
can't uncut the cords in my own mind.
Camaros and caramel, sweet and sad,
the life I lost to the one I had.

3:16 P.M.
LYRICAL COUPLETS

Keys hit the counter with a hollow click,
coat on the chair, breath slow, bones sick.
Curtains closed to cut the glare,
crawl through the quiet, collapse in the chair.

Mind's still mired in the mud we stirred,
every memory sharp as a slivered word.
Clock's got claws, it drags the day,
pulling my pulse in a leaden sway.

Shoes still tied, I can't unlatch,
eyes half-closed like a broken latch.
The hum of the fridge feels like a hymn,
singing me under, pulling me in.

Tomorrow's teeth are at my door,
I can't stand, but I can't ignore.
Pillow's a promise I almost keep,
3:16 PM, post therapy -
I just want to sleep.

Orbiting
FREE VERSE

The silence swallows sound before it's born,
and light bends wrong around my skin.
Every breath is thin as glass in winter,
every shadow a slow collapse inward.

I drift where the dark eats its own tail,
a spiral drawn by hands I cannot see.
The stars are teeth - white and waiting -
and I am their patient, unwilling meal.

Your voice comes through in fractured waves,
each word molten, burning the air between us.
I reach, but the distance blooms like a bruise,
a violet ache skewered to my ribs.

Heat rises, closer now, the crown of the sun,
my blood a tide against the pull.
Skin prickles with the scent of fire and iron,
and I wonder which will take me first -
the burn, or the breath I cannot catch.

Gravity clenches its fist around my lungs,
and the silence closes in, absolute.
I am not falling,
I am not flying,
I am only orbiting -
and the star is winning.

Hymn for the Wrong Kind of Boy
FREE VERSE

i didn't want to need this -
but i showed up anyway.

he wasn't cruel.
he looked like someone who might hurt me -
but didn't.

i needed a reason
to leave the apartment
that wasn't groceries, or bills,
or pretending i had somewhere to be.

the elevator groans
like it's holding pressure instead of people -
and i take it anyway.
the stairs punish my joints.
the windows turn my breath shallow.
i hate heights -
and i go up there
on purpose
every week.
and somehow,
that changed me
more than i ever saw coming.

i sit in the same waiting room chair:
the one furthest from the door,
nearest the hall that opens into him.
no one's usually next to me.
no one's across.
but i sit there like it's carved out for me -
like the pattern matters more than the comfort.

i text him early,
like i'm apologizing
for being a burden;
for being on time;
for existing at all.

i sit on the couch - always the couch.
never the hammock chairs.
i don't trust the weight.
not of the chairs.
not of me.

what meets me in that room
doesn't ask for anything.
nothing cracks beneath my weight -
not the seat,
not the silence,
not him.

i still think
this could all collapse.
not because he's failed me -
but because i've been trained to expect the fall.

he says not to judge him on my fears -
but by his actions.
and i try.
but when your history is a blueprint of betrayal,
you flinch -
before the hand even moves.

i gave him
the blood-spattered backlog:
that little black book
full of things i never meant to share.
and he read it.
all of it.
he didn't flinch.
he called it a kindness -
like i wasn't a lost cause.
like i wasn't wasting his time.

he reminds me -
in posture, and tone, and haircut -
of a kind of man
i learned to be afraid of.
he looks like the enemy.
and i've told him that.

he's married.
he's religious.
i'm not.

i've been burned too many times
by people who claimed
to speak for god.

and still -
somehow -
this works.

he sees under the surface
into the place where i've locked
the nine-year-old version of me
inside a cell of wires and whispering static.
no light.
no key.
just memory and noise.
and somehow, he doesn't look away.
he doesn't flinch from the dark -
he just stays.

when he reflects me back,
it doesn't feel distorted.
i don't ask for validation,
but he offers it anyway -
and it lands
like silence without shame.

i bring him the mess -
the ink-blurred pages,
the pieces i want fixed
but don't know how to hand over.
not for praise.
not to be saved.
just so he knows
what he's helping carry.

i'm letting him in.
i want him to see
what no one else ever has.
i'm not holding back.

i don't have this connection
with anyone else.
never have.
don't think i ever will again.
and no -
it's not love, or lust.

it's not confusion.
it's just
real.
and rare.
and impossible to explain
without sounding like i'm asking for more
than i am.

i don't always want to open up.
i don't always believe
this is going to hold.

trusting him
feels like flexing a long-dead muscle -
it hurts in a way that might be good,
but still hurts.
and the pull inside me says:
this is how you fell last time.
this is how deep it cut,
when you believed.
i don't want to trust him less.
but some days it feels like
the other shoe is already midair,
and i'm bracing for the impact.

but i keep showing up.
i keep opening.
i keep trying.

i want this to work.
and it is working -
even when it's hard.
even when it shouldn't.

but what if one day
he isn't there?
what if the room opens
and it's someone else?
or no one else.
and it's over.

i don't know how to thank him
without making it sound like goodbye.

and maybe that's not strength.
maybe it's something closer to faith -
not the kind he believes in,
but the kind i invent
every time i walk through that door
to sing a hymn i was never taught
for the wrong kind of boy.
and mean every note.

Faces in the Closet
FREE VERSE

They do not knock.

They do not wait;
they are already here
when I close my eyes.

Breath on the back of my neck -
hot, sour,
memory-shaped.

Fingers curling in the dark
around the doorknob of my skull.

I have locked them in,
but the key is mine,
and I keep turning
without meaning to.

Some still wear the faces I remember.

Some wear the faces I gave them
in nightmares when their real ones rotted.

All of them look at me
like I never left that room.

That bed.

That hospital room.

That prison.

They whisper with mouths full of dust.

They stand in corners
the light refuses to touch.

And I wonder,
if I burn the house down,
will they follow me out?

The Picnic Table
EXPERIMENTAL EMDR EXPERIENCE POEM

Close your eyes.
Take a deep breath in and hold it.
Now let it out.
Good.

Let's begin.

Left. Right. Left. Right.
Left. Right. Left. Right.

Left. Right. Left. Right.
Are the buzzers okay, too strong, too weak?
Left. Right. Left. Right.
Another deep breath, let it out, don't peek.

Left. Right. Left. Right.
Feel the hum settle into your hands.
Left. Right. Left. Right.
Now pull it back, through the shifting sands.

Left. Right. Left. Right.
To the kitchen table where the shouting grew.
Left. Right. Left. Right.
To the locked-door nights where fear still blew.

Left. Right. Left. Right.
The shadow of one I once called my friend.
Left. Right. Left. Right.
Words that cut deep and refused to bend.

Left. Right. Left. Right.
Now the picnic table waits for you in the sun…
Left. Right. Left. Right.
Splinters biting where your small hands once run.

Left. Right. Left. Right.
Nine-year-old self sits across the grain.
Left. Right. Left. Right.
Eyes like the storm before summer rain.

Left. Right. Left. Right.
Tell him the truth: you will not be alone.
Left. Right. Left. Right.
Though the years ahead will grind you to bone.

Left. Right. Left. Right.
Ask him to speak, when the time is right.
Left. Right. Left. Right.
He nods, he stands, and walks into night.

Left. Right. Left. Right.
The hum fades down to a whispering stream.
Left. Right. Left. Right.
The present returns like a dim-willed dream.

Left. Right. Left. Right.
Now open your eyes, you're here, you're awake.
Left. Right. Left. Right.
The weight is still yours, but it's lighter to take.

Left. Right. Left. Right.
Left. Right. Left. Right.

Stop.

Same time, next week.

Progress Report
VILLANELLE

I swear I'm standing still, though I move each day.
The road feels endless, the horizon blurred,
Yet something inside keeps clearing the way.

I trip on the stones that memory lays,
Old wounds whisper louder than what I've heard,
I swear I'm standing still, though I move each day.

These steps are smaller than I wished they'd weigh,
My victories quiet, my courage slurred,
Yet something inside keeps clearing the way.

The storms still batter, the nights still betray,
But roots keep holding though the sky's deterred,
I swear I'm standing still, though I move each day.

Even the shadows can't force me to stray,
Though hope feels fragile, a trembling word,
Yet something inside keeps clearing the way.

The past still pulls, but it cannot stay,
A seed is still a seed, though undisturbed,
I swear I'm standing still, though I move each day,
Yet something inside keeps clearing the way.

Day 1057
FREE VERSE

I didn't think I would come back.
I swore I didn't need it.
But here I am, counting my own breaths
like coins in an empty pocket,
waiting for the signal to shut my eyes.

The couch moans when I settle into it,
a sound older than my body,
older than my grief.
The buzzers are slick in my hands,
as if they know the story
I don't want to tell.

We go in slow.
The smell of cigarette smoke in the garage.
Her laugh -
sharp, cracked,
still somehow beautiful.
The sting in my chest
when I realize I can't touch her,
not even here.

Her voice asks questions
I pretend not to hear,
because answering means opening the door
to the part of me that still believes
I could have saved her,
but I answer anyway.

The hum softens.
The room comes back into focus.
I am not crying, but I should be.
I am not speaking, but I should be.
And the silence feels heavier
than anything I said out loud.

By the time I leave,
the hallway smells like antiseptic and rain.
I've carried her ghost in both hands
and set it back down in the same place.

Monday, August 4th. 2:00 P.M.
Central Standard Time.
Day 1057.
Still breathing.
Still here.

Therapy Session
ROCK BALLAD

I walk in with my armor up,
every week, same couch and chair.
Desk holds a cross I don't believe,
and you always meet me there.
You've got a southern smile like a Sunday hymn,
and I've got scars from the sermon's fire.
I'm trying to trust in a stranger's eyes,
when religion's my funeral pyre.

You say, "Judge me by my actions,
not the ghosts you've come to know."
And I want to believe that you mean it -
but belief has far to go.

So I sit down,
and I tear myself open.
You write nothing down,
like the truth's just been spoken.
Every word's a gamble,
every silence a confession -
And I keep coming back,
to another therapy session.

You're a year from my own face,
but you've got a life I've never had.
A family, faith, a Sunday suit,
and I've got shadows that have driven me mad.
I hate the hymns but I hear your voice,
telling me pain's not a life sentence.
But I've heard promises dressed like hope -
and I've paid the price for repentance.

You say, "Judge me by my actions,
not the names you've learned to curse."
And I want to believe that you're different -
but the past still makes it worse.

So I sit down,
and I tear myself open.
You write nothing down,
like the truth's just been spoken.
Every word's a gamble,
every silence a confession -

And I keep coming back,
to another therapy session.

Even when I want to vanish,
even when I can't speak clear…
I keep walking through that doorway,
'cause I'm terrified to disappear…
You tell me that the trying counts,
but the weight still breaks my spine…
I don't know if you can save me,
and I can't stop drawing the line…

So I sit down,
and I tear myself wide open.
You write nothing down,
like the truth's all just been spoken.
Every word's a gamble,
every silence my dark confession -
And I keep coming back,
I keep crawling back,
to another therapy session.

One more hour,
one more try…
'Cause if I stop -
then it's going to be
goodbye.

X

The Green Shoots from Ruin
TERZA RIMA

From shattered glass, I watch the soft stems rise,
a tender green against the ash and stone,
small proof that even endings hold surprise.

The frost still clings, the wind still cuts the bone,
yet roots push deeper where the ground once broke,
and cracks now cradle seeds they would have thrown.

Each day, a leaf unfolds, a word is spoke
that once was locked behind a tongue of grief,
while sunlight filters through the dark like smoke.

It's not a cure - it's not a grand relief -
but in the rubble, life has found its hue,
and in my chest, a breath that's green and brief.

Though storms may come, they'll meet what's growing new,
for ruin is the soil where hope takes root,
and I am learning what these hands can do.

I Survive
ANTHEM VERSE

Cut me down, I'll rise from the ruin,
Skin still scarred, but my heart keeps movin'.
Every wound just writes another line,
in the story that's already mine.

You throw stones, I turn them to towers,
Count the nights, I still claim the hours.
You can burn my sky, block my light -
I'll paint the stars back into the night.

Tried to break me, tried to chain me,
Every fall just re-engrained me.
If the world wants war, I'll drive -

I survive - through the fire, through the flood,
I survive - through the venom in the blood.
You can drown me deep, you can cut me wide,
I will rise from the wreckage every time -
I survive.

You said "stay down," I learned to stand taller,
Echoed screams just make my voice holler.
Every crack shadow only sharpened the blame,
and I'm not dying to play your game.

I've been nailed to walls made of sin's sorrow,
Still I claw on toward my own day tomorrow.
The ground can quake, but I don't bow -
I've made my peace, and I took my vow.

Tried to blind me, tried to bind me,
Still the road ahead will find me.
If the dark won't bend, I'll drive -

I survive - through the fire, through the flood,
I survive - through the venom in the blood.
You can drown me deep, you can cut me wide,
I will rise from the wreckage every time -
I survive.

Every scar is a seed I've drawn in fire,
Every breath's a spark, a steel-cage choir.
Every fall I've turned into midnight flight,
Every loss I've dragged into morning light.

I survive - through the fire, through the flood,
I survive - through the venom in the blood.
You can drown me deep, you can cut me wide,
I will rise from the wreckage every time -
I survive, I survive, I survive -
And I'm still alive.

I survive - through the fire, through the flood,
I survive - through the venom in the blood.
You can drown me deep, you can cut me wide,
I will rise from the wreckage every time -
I survive.

Four Letter Words
FREE VERSE

I've said 'em all.
The ones you whisper in back alleys.
The ones that get you sent out of church,
slammed out of family dinners,
blocked, muted, erased.

I've spit them in traffic,
hissed them into the dark,
thrown them like glass bottles
just to watch something shatter
that isn't me.

Hell, damn, fuck, shit -
the alphabet of my bad days.
Every syllable another brick
I stack between me and the ones
who might still give a damn.

And yeah… even love.
Love's a four-letter word when you can't
stand your own reflection.
When it lands in your mouth
like a hot coal,
and you don't know whether to hold it
or spit it out before it burns.

But I keep saying them.
Every bitter, bleeding word.
Because they're mine.
Because they're the only language
I've got left that feels real.

And if it hurts to hear them -
good.
It should.

What the Fire Knows
FREE VERSE

I sit –
palms open, heart
uncertain,
ink-heavy veins
pulsing questions –
when I sat cross-legged
beneath the kitchen table,
spiral notebook pressed hard against my knees,
pen scratching with insistence,
drowning out the shouting.

The solitary desk waits,
scarred with doubts,
burned and rebuilt,
pages half-written,
whispers of wings
waiting in margins.

My mother's voice
soft rain -
choose safety, choose sense -
my father's silence
thunder in an empty wood and
the drought that follows.

My lover's fingerprints
bruise me still,
throat
tight with quieted truths -
the world's hands
pressed over my mouth,
each false friendship
another stone
sewn into my pockets,
sinking.

Yet something
deeper than survival
calls me, more
insistent
than fear's seduction
or shame's familiar embrace -
something coded

in bone,
in marrow,
the instinctive ache
of a pen tethered,
the dam buckling
beneath parchment tides.

I know -
I've always known -
I was made from words,
born to build worlds
from ashes,
to speak fire
without apology.

What if -
what if the loneliness
becomes sanctuary,
the silence,
hewing fertile soil?

What if the act of creating
is not rebellion,
but respiration -
breathing out stories,
inhaling hope?

The chains were never iron,
just brittle whispers
from lips untrusted,
rusted shadows
beneath kitchen tables
I can break
with a single sentence,
a trembling phrase
that remembers
its own strength.

So today,
not tomorrow —
but what if these veins clot —
but what if
the words choke and crumble —
but what if
even worse,
I don't —

I hold this pen -
warm from hesitation, heavy with ink -
as answered prayer,
filled with dark pigment
pulled from my ink-laden body,
I write myself
onto empty pages,
stitching trauma into tapestries
of fierce,
fragile beauty.

But today - today I choose
the burning desk,
the pen that bleeds truth,
the wings unfolding -
quietly, with the warmth on my fingertips
and the certain
uncertain freedom
of becoming
who the fire knows
I've always been.

Rabbit Foot
HAIKU

Scars are bleeding dry,
after everything I've seen;
I'm the rabbit's foot.

Win Again
SONNET

Upon this field where fate hath struck me low,
And oft hath cast my crown into the dust,
I wander, weighed with wounds the years bestow,
Bereft of kith, of coin, of sworn-held trust.

The cup of loss, I've drained it to its lees,
Its bitter dregs have scalded soul and bone;
The storms have stripped the blossom from my trees,
And left me barren, cold, and all alone.

Yet still, though night devours the waning shame,
Some ember hides within the ash's hue;
If but one triumph dares to call my name,
This weary heart might beat with strength anew.

So grant me, gods, though deaf to pleas they've been,
One final chance to fight - and win again.

Swallowed
PANTOUM

I've swallowed my pride, and it burned on the way,
The venom I carried now fading to dust,
I've eaten the nights when I could not stay,
And fed on the bones of the things I mistrust.

The venom I carried now fading to dust,
Each ember of anger dissolved on my tongue,
And fed on the bones of the things I mistrust,
Till hunger grew tired of the battles I've sung.

Each ember of anger dissolved on my tongue,
I've eaten the nights when my spirit would weep,
Till hunger grew tired of the battles I've sung,
And silence came calling to cradle my sleep.

I've eaten the nights when my spirit would weep,
I've swallowed my pride, and it burned on the way,
And silence came calling to cradle my sleep,
I've eaten the nights when I could not stay.

Start Breathing
TRIOLET

When you don't know what else to do, start breathing.
The night feels endless, cold, and far too near.
Through shadows deep, the smallest hope is seething.
When you don't know what else to do, start breathing.
The heart still beats, though quiet in its grieving,
A fragile thread that keeps you tethered here.
When you don't know what else to do, start breathing.
The night feels endless, cold, and far too near.

Procession of a Funeral
BALLAD

The fiddles start their weeping,
the drums keep steady time,
we march the road to daylight's end
and leave the past behind.

We carry what once bound us,
in caskets carved of oak,
and cast the key to earth's deep mouth
beneath the evening's cloak.

The mourners wear their colors,
the jesters wear their grin,
we bury every grief we wore
and seal it deep within.

The road ahead grows golden,
the tavern door swings wide,
we toast the ghosts that could not keep
their claws in us this ride.

The Heirloom
TAVERN SONG

She came to us in summer's bloom,
a friend of blood, though not by name.
We passed her down, our prized heirloom,
as seasons turned, she stayed the same.

So lift the glass, and let it ring,
for heirlooms lost to wandering.

First hers to guard, then mine to keep,
through autumn dusk and winter's light.
We laughed through days, we drank through deep,
and held her close against the night.

So lift the glass, and let it ring,
for heirlooms lost to wandering.

But years unspooled and threads grew thin,
the loom unworked, the hands withdrew.
The ties that bound were worn within,
and faded out of time's own view.

So lift the glass, and let it ring,
for heirlooms lost to wandering.

I pray she warms some hearth tonight,
a treasured gift in someone's care.
For though she's gone beyond my sight,
my heart still keeps her shining there.

So lift the glass, and let it ring,
for heirlooms lost to wandering.

Salve of Sunlight
LYRICAL VERSE

Through thistle and thorn, by the tide's tender turning,
where winds weave their whispers through willow and wain,
I wandered in woe, with the frost in me burning,
till dawn's dappled fingers unfastened the chain.

A sliver of gold in the gray sky was gleaming,
it spilled on the stones where the shadows still lay,
and sudden my soul, from its sorrowful dreaming,
was lifted and lit by the balm of the day.

O bright is the breath of the morning's first measure,
it carries the kiss of the meadow and moor,
it gathers the grief and it trades it for treasure,
it opens the heart like an unguarded door.

So seek ye the spill of the sun on the water,
and follow the fire where the far hills ignite;
the darker the night, aye, the dearer the slaughter -
the sweeter the salve in the arms of the light.

This Poem is a Trapdoor
FREE VERSE

It begins in shadow,
thick as syrup on the walls,
the kind that drips slow
and makes you wonder
if the house is bleeding.

Footsteps creak overhead;
someone is here,
someone is always here,
waiting with madness and molars
in the dark.

The windows are blacked out,
the air smells like rain-soaked crust,
and somewhere in the attic,
a voice whispers my name,
low and careful,
like it knows how fragile my ribs are.

Every word in this poem
is leading you closer;
you don't know what it is yet,
but you've been clutching the railing
the whole way down the stairs.

And then you open the door.

Surprise.

You're safe.

And the Garden Grew Anyway
VICTORY ANTHEM

The frost rolled in on a silver night,
Turned the morning fields to white,
We thought the bloom was gone for good,
No sun could break that frozen wood.
But deep below in the sleeping clay,
A stubborn seed still found its way,
Pushed on through the cold and grey,
And the garden grew anyway.

And the garden grew anyway,
Through the thorns and through decay,
Though the storms would come to stay,
Still the colors found their play.
Life will rise where it may,
And the garden grew anyway.

The weeds came fast with a reckless speed,
Tangling tight around each seed,
The roses bled with a velvet tear,
The lilies swayed in the heavy air.
The bees still danced on a summer tune,
The marigolds kissed the heat of noon,
Even shadows could not dismay,
For the garden grew anyway.

And the garden grew anyway,
Through the thorns and through decay,
Though the storms would come to stay,
Still the colors found their play.
Life will rise where it may,
And the garden grew anyway.

Even in winter's cold command,
Roots reach out through the sleeping land,
Dreaming of rain, of the gentle light,
Holding their ground in the deepest night.
We may fall, we may bend, we may break apart,
But something still grows in the quiet heart,
It's the stubborn truth we can't betray -
The garden grows anyway.

And I've been lost in the barren years,
Sowed my hopes in a field of fears,
But I've seen green in the strangest place,
Found my faith in a flower's face.
It doesn't wait for the world to smile,
It finds its road through the rocky mile,
And I'll learn to live like the blooms in May,
For the garden grows anyway.

And the garden grew anyway,
Through the thorns and through decay,
Though the storms would come to stay,
Still the colors found their play.
Life will rise where it may,
And the garden grew anyway.

So I'll take my root in the soil today,
Come what will, come what may,
And if I bloom or fade to grey -
The garden grows anyway.

After

Dear Joseph
SUMMATION VERSE

You've bled in the garden,
    and still, the flowers came.
You've buried your ghosts,
    marched them past the gates,
    and still, they sang in your ear.

You've loved wrong,
    loved late,
    loved the ones who left,
    and cursed yourself for being left at all.

You've swallowed pride,
    fear,
    hatred,
    until your gut was nothing but acid,
    until your spine bent like the branches of winter.

You've prayed to gods you don't believe in,
    cursed their silence,
    and still searched for their eyes in the ceiling cracks.

You've been the bruise,
    the cracked glass,
    the shadow on the wall.

You've been the rabbit's foot,
    lucky just to wake up,
    cursed to count every pill.

You've danced in taverns of your own mind,
    sung dirges for the boy you never became,
    the man you couldn't save,
    the faces you see in the closet when the lights go out.

And still -
    still you survived.

But survival is not the crown.

It is the floor.

And you've been lying on it too damn long.

Here's the truth, Joseph:
    If you rot, it's on you.
    If you fade,
        it's your hand on the dimmer.
    If you choke,
        it's because you never opened your mouth.

This is your life -
    stitched from scars,
    poured from pills,
    measured in losses,
    and lit by the thin light of mornings
    you didn't think you'd see.

It's ugly.

It's broken.

It's yours.

So shut up.

Get up.
Do something with it.
Bleed on the page.
Bite the hand that holds you back.

Plant the goddamn seed.

And the garden -
your garden -
will grow anyway.

About the Author

Joseph Brindley is a poet and fiction writer whose work navigates the boundaries of grief, trauma, and personal transformation. He is currently pursuing his Master of Fine Arts (MFA) in Creative Writing and has dedicated his life to telling stories that will truly sing to someone. To him, storytelling is almost spiritual, where the fiction can show the truth more clearly than any honest work.

When not writing, he's working through therapy and toward the next project, always forming in the back of his head. His life is shaped by the people who are still here, alongside those who are not. He's the proud uncle of two beautiful nieces, is a younger brother to a woman four years older, and is the son of parents who are long gone but still linger in these pages.

This is his debut poetry collection.

Coming 2026

Inanitas
Poetry Collection II

By Joseph Brindley

Connect with Me

I'd love to hear from readers and fellow writers.

Website
www.josephbrindley.com

Updated Social Links
can be found there
on the Contact Page.

www.ingramcontent.com/pod-product-compliance
Lightning Source LLC
Chambersburg PA
CBHW022101090426
42743CB00008B/679